Martial Art Over 50

One Man's Dream

The Inner Aspect

James Killingsworth

Acknowledgements

On this page I wish to convey my deepest thanks to everyone who contributed to the growth and development of our being in martial art and especially taekwondo. Like on a journey, many of us have walked together for a while. I have been so humbled to have shared the only thing I really have, time. It is said that the only activity that will give you any real and lasting intrinsic value is being with those whom you wish to spend that time together. Each of you has deposited something of value in me that is truly esoteric and no longer is it subject to the decay of time. It is written in the starlight. May all your journeys begin and end in freedom.

Every step you have ever taken,
has lead you to
where you are now.

1. Eternal Grand Master H. U. Lee, for the creation of the ATA, American Taekwondo Association.

2. The American Taekwondo Association, for allowing people fifty years and older to practice taekwondo and for the formulation of the Ten Attributes.

3. Chief Master Mark Sustaire, for placing great emphasis on flexibility training.

4. Senior Master Sam Phrumjuntun, who embodied the kind of man I wanted to be in martial art.

5. Mr. Brian and Ms. Dana Rogers, our first taekwondo instructors.

6. Master Randy Carvin, who taught me how to relax during sparring.

7. Master Don May, who taught me to "kick high."

8. Mrs. Kathleen Flatt, who taught me "strategy" in sparring.

9. Mr. Frank Haslip, our second instructor.

10. Master Michael Pak, our third instructor.

11. Mrs. Susan Menchaca.

12. My wife Sherry Killingsworth, fourth degree black belt, who shared my journey in taekwondo and was my best sparring partner.

13. My children, Laura and Joey Killingsworth, who were always two belts ahead of Sherry and I in our color belt journey and helped to teach us martial art. Together we were the first Black Belt Family in our local ATA School.

14. Miss Jessica Preston, who proof read my manuscript.

15. My tournament competitors, who raised my level to the Top Ten competition and World Champion. I bow before them and thank them with all of my heart and my being.

    Mr. Jerry Liming

    Mr. Rodney Tooley

    Mr. Doug McConnaughhay

    Mr. Bill Matlock

    Master Gerald Frentz

    Master Lorne Davidson

    Master Jay Martin

    Master Chuck Sears

    Mr. Peter Robustelli

    Mr. Tony D'Anglelo

    Mr. Mike Samples

    Mr. Pat Sivalingam

There are no Masters of
old age,
only students.

From The Author

This book has been written for the benefit of those men and women who wish to practice martial art and particularly taekwondo in their later years. These are to me, the most remarkable people. I have known many. The wish to grow in the sense of being and to strive to find out about yourself within the crucible of martial art is a very high aim.

Most people at age fifty or older are winding down their lives, becoming more sedentary and relinquishing their remaining potential to the relentless reclamation forces of Mother Nature. But to those who wish more from life and are striving to develop their individuality under the auspices of martial art, it is to you that I speak. It is to you that I bow and acknowledge this high aim and the path that I have traveled.

Although this book is primarily for seniors who begin martial art late in life, the principles therein can be useful even for those who have practiced since childhood. For time passes through all of us and we are all students in the aging process. In fact, this journey for seniors can be even more rewarding than for young people in the sense that it is much more difficult without youth. For instead of youth, seniors have to overcome two obstacles. The first obstacle is all of the difficulties that are associated with the practice of martial art. The second obstacle is all the difficulties that are associated with the aging process.

The contents of this book will reflect the uniqueness of my background in life. Being a pharmacist by profession, with degrees in biology and chemistry, I have devoted many years of service to the sick, the aged and dying. That has instilled in me a deep desire to understand the aging process and how to retard it. In this book, nutrition, injuries, training, yoga, meditation and many other aspects of martial art are explored from the perspective of achieving a major aim in one's life. In addition, my participation in esoteric groups over many years has revealed to me *inner knowledge* of the laws of the body, mind and feelings and the importance of their continued growth.

To most people, the horizontal or external aspect of martial art is all they will ever know. Yet to a few, there is a great yearning to penetrate the external and seek the essence, or inner aspect. These people have a deep longing to understand their life and to grow as a human should, as a self-evolving creature. This is vertical development or *self-individuality*.

To be sure, there must be a balance between the outer and inner aspects. It is this balance I strive to elucidate in this book. It is my wish that martial art can penetrate your essence and open you up to knowledge and understanding of a *deeper level of being*.

Come now, we have much to do

Table of Contents

Lighting the Pilot Light 2

Nutrition.. 18

Flexibility and Stretching 42

Injuries 74

The Law of Effort... 98

Acceleration 112

Explosiveness 126

Plyometric Training.. 132

Targeting 148

My Style of Sparring 154

The Sparring Mind (Simultaneity) 162

The Value of Forms.. 179

The Organ of Sense 193

The Role of Music in Martial Art....................................... 202

Tournament Preparation.. 209

Meditations 220

About the Author... 227

Appendix/Bibliography.. 235

Chapter 1

*The Ocean does not
interfere with
the water.*

The Diagram of Human Potential

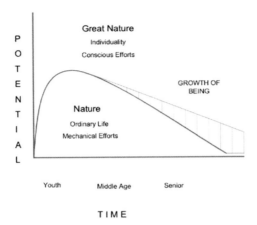

Lighting the Pilot Light

You must accept yourself. Mother Nature no longer needs you to continue the human race. You have procreated and your children are almost grown and independent. You are past your prime. You are still powerful and capable. But also, you are probably out of shape. Maybe you eat too much and eat the foods that are not good for you. You eat for taste and not to nourish your body. It could be that you drink too much or indulge in other pastimes that do not contribute to your growth as a human being. You still have to work every day and it is difficult to find time to train. You notice that your once slim waistline now has a bulge that will not go away. When you do exercise you find it difficult to get going and aren't quite sure what to do. Perhaps you were a runner in the past, lifted weights or played one or more sports. When you do go to the gym or to the track, your plan for training is vague. Perhaps you saw a movie last night and it inspired you to work out. Maybe you were shamed by the view of yourself in the mirror, or your partner or friend let a comment slip about your less-than-youthful shape. Or it could be that it is New Year's Eve and you are like others who believe in the miracle of resolution. You live vicariously through those you watch playing sports on TV. When you do work out, you revert to your mechanical ways and do too much, too soon. Because your body is not ready you overdo it. You become terribly sore, aggravate an old injury or cause a new one. You wake up the next day and your inspiration is gone, so you force yourself. Your workout is not fun. It is boring, painful and you damage your body further. In disgust, you want to give up. Finally, the promise you made to one part of yourself the night before, to wake up and run or exercise, is received by another part of yourself in the morning, and it wants to sleep more. The wonderful human being next to you is warm and soft, and the promise of the night before is lost in the power of comfort. This type of cycle slowly continues until your envelope of mental, physical and emotional capability contracts. The possibilities for your life become more and more limited. It does not seem like there is anything inside of you that can repulse the relentless reclamation forces of Mother Nature. Gradually, you passively accept the aging process as an inevitable path and lose the initiative to grow as a human being.

This is the situation I found myself in.

What could be ahead?

The potential for human development by the practice of martial art is great. The physical body will gradually become more flexible. After a year or two, it will probably become more flexible than ever before in your life. Your muscles will become bands of steel and will grow in strength, quickness and power. Your body will become faster than thought or perception. You will become almost prehensile with your legs and feet. You will improve in your anaerobic endurance and ability to exercise. You will become extremely healthy. Eventually your body will become what it should be - *your servant.*

"Here I was given something I could do day, after day, after day...
I had my own body...I never could even get rid of it... it could teach me...
the teacher was with me as my body and in this behavior form I could
*become educated." —*W. A. NYLAND.

Martial art is one of the few things I have found in this life that develops one's feeling center. There are no "schools" for its development in ordinary life. While the body is fully formed physically, the feeling center is only half-developed. Feelings give aliveness to the body. Martial art gives quality and spirit to the postures and movement of the body. Self-control is the aim. The practice of forms (sequenced postures and movements) creates a potent motivating force and an inner harmony between the three centers. Real emotion begins when you strive to make the body perform specific movements and postures and blend them together to produce a configuration of beauty and harmony. The feelings will transform into a motivating force that will create a *wish* to reach the aim you have set for yourself in life. Gradually, the wish of the feeling center will grow into the greatest emotional development of all - a real conscience. Your petty likes and dislikes will dissolve and reform into the great potentiality of the feeling center - *inspiration, aspiration, silence* and *conscience.*

Your mental capacity and capability will grow in many unique and unusual ways. Martial art will stimulate the growth of other parts of your brain that are rarely exercised or developed in our culture. Some call these functions of the "right brain." Your mental faculties will grow in spatial perception, mentation by form (body memory), attention and awareness. Instead of unrelenting inner dialog, your mind will become clear. Gradually, over a period of time, the mind will be able to *direct* the body. The *director,* as it is called, is a higher function for the mind. It has the capability of precise control over the body. This function will orient you toward a lifelong goal of major importance. Eventually, the highest function of the mind will be discovered, that is-*self-awareness.* Your level of being will change forever.

You will make lifelong friends in martial art. As you come up through the ranks, deep friendships will form with those who train with you. You will begin to realize the value of those who share the same aim with you. As a middle-aged or senior student, you will train alongside younger people. Most of them will accept you as a fellow student, sharing in the exertion of training. You will learn as much from these young ones as you learn from your instructor.

There is much more, as you will see.

Some Principles to Understand

From the time of your birth, your body, feelings and mind have developed without your conscious effort. The body has matured, and really all you had to do was feed and water it and keep it clean and warm. The body's desires of hunger, thirst, heat, cold, pain and pleasure have reminded you to take care of it.

The growth of feelings have been developed haphazardly, without any plan or direction. Most of these feelings mimic your parental and peer influences and continue to this day. Similar to a forgotten orphan, the feelings use the body for its playground. Likes, dislikes, love, hate, euphoria, anger, hurt, melancholy, exhilaration, jealousy and a myriad of petty little feelings romp unopposed to the tune of external impressions. There are no schools or universities devoted to the growth and development of the feeling center. Your "emotional body" is roughly half-developed and is a mess of opposites in constant change.

If the emotional body is half-developed, your intellectual body is almost totally undeveloped. It is stuffed with all kinds of facts and figures from the "educational process" it has passed through. You may even be a professional and have really got down to "brass tacks" in some particular area of subjective learning. Now you know a whole lot about very little. Basically, the education of the intellect is merely the functioning of the *formatory apparatus*. This apparatus is called such because of its mechanical nature, which means that the same thought processes continually repeat themselves over and over again. It is continually anticipating the future and recollecting the past. It is never now. You cannot stop it, no matter how stupid or idiotic your thoughts are. Recurring thoughts are drunk with imagination, full of untruthful pictures of yourself and accounts against others that did not treat you right. This apparatus identifies with everything. This function is the center of internal considering, which consists of self-justification, acquired opinions and pictures of yourself that has little to do with reality. It is sometimes called "singing your song" or inner dialog.

All of this previous growth has really been without your conscious effort, for *youth* has been the great active force in your life. Now that you have passed your prime, no longer does youth support your body, feelings or intellect.

In order to grow at this stage of life, one must *transform the mechanicalness of youth into a conscious striving toward a meaningful aim for your life*. Without this understanding, there can be only one result. You will grow old according to Mother Nature's whim, and she will have her way with you.

In accordance, you must also understand that for any given training session, you cannot just "jump right into it." You cannot go from ground zero to performing the perfect form or engaging in tournament sparring like you could when you were young. You will damage yourself. You need to warm up and prepare yourself for that which you wish to practice. You need to *raise your level of preparedness and develop your capacity for doing*. This is what I call *lighting the pilot light*.

You understand that when you get into your car on a cold day, you must start it and let it warm up to operating temperature before you depart. If you do not do this on a regular basis, then your car's engine will wear faster. Some parts will warm faster than others, thereby exerting pressure on the cold ones before they are ready to operate. These parts eventually become damaged and their performance suffers. Suppose that each time you wanted to take a hot shower, you had to go out into the garage and light the water heater. Then you had to wait for it to get hot. Of course you don't have to do that. That is why you have a pilot light. The pilot light keeps the water hot by way of a thermostat, which is set to keep the water in the tank at a certain temperature. When the hot water is needed, it simply flows. The pilot light is ready to light the big burner and keep the water hot when it flows. When you are ready to shower, you simply turn on the hot water.

In martial art, your pilot light is the *wish* to bring the body into a state of preparedness so that it can perform *without warming up* and without damaging itself. This wish is different than a desire or a "want." Wants or desires have no lasting value. They disappear after being satisfied and have no perseverance. They send you right back to ground zero each time, mechanically repeating themselves in an endless cycle. A *wish* is a persevering state, the practice of which, day in and day out, raises your level of being, your level of preparedness, your level of capability and participation. The thermostat in you is called *self-remembering* or the *reminding factor*. When this reminding factor lives inside of you, it reconciles the aim you have set for yourself and the retarding factors that oppose this aim. It remembers what you said you wanted to attain and questions what you are doing now in relation to that statement. It shortens the distance between what you think or say and what you do. This constant remembering of the aim you have set for yourself will introduce the question of the purpose of your life. This question is the reconciling force of your life - it is your *conscience*. Your conscience is responsible for reducing the space between what you say, and what you do.

> *"Is this, what I do now, in conformity with the aim*
> *I have set for myself, or is it not?"* —W. A. NYLAND.

This is what is required if you wish to grow in martial arts after fifty. A man with a pilot light and a thermostat is a man who stands on his own two feet, firmly rooted in the ground. There he lifts his face to the heavens, his arms outstretched, reaching for his destiny. Light your pilot light. Here is how I lit mine.

Everything Falls to its Nearest Stability

Martial art is nearly impossible with a bad back. The back is the center of all bodily movement. Not only must it support the body by repulsing the eternal effects of gravity, but all movement begins with the stability of the back supporting the leverage of the arms and legs. If your back is not ready for these postures and movements, then you will destroy your journey before you even begin. Of equal importance are the spinal nerves that innervate every organ and muscle. Without proper flexibility and strength of the back musculature, all martial art techniques will suffer, and your striving will only reach a certain threshold. Without necessary nerve innervation, you will not obtain the self-control to execute techniques with the attributes that render them effective. Just as the back is important for martial art, the abdomen is also important. The abdomen braces the back and allows it to absorb the tremendous stresses placed on it by kicking, blocking and striking. The abdominal, intercostal and back muscles raise, extend and withdraw your kicks. It is said that the life force issues from your abdomen, just below the navel. The back and abdomen are two levels of the foundation upon which you will build your house in martial art. Once solidified, this foundation may never need attention again except after injury, disease or long absence. Therefore, strike the first match that will light your pilot light and raise the back and abdomen to a critical level of development.

Be careful with the following exercises. Ask your doctor if you are healthy enough to engage in the activities listed below. If you have any acute pain while doing these postures or movements, stop and reconsider if they are for you.

The Eye of Revelation

When I was a young man, my stepfather gave me a small pamphlet that was some forty pages long. It was called *The Eye of Revelation: The Ancient Tibetan Rites of Rejuvenation*, published in 1924. It was in the form of a narrative written by a retired British officer named Peter Kelder. After retiring from service, he returned to the Himalayan Mountains where he served. On his journey, he was admitted into a Tibetan Monastery, where he was amazed at the youthful look and abilities of the monks. He was able to observe certain rituals that were practiced by the monks every day. The monks said that this was their "fountain of youth" and called them Rites.

Over the years, I have practiced these Rites several times, especially when I was recovering from a major injury or returning to martial art after a long absence. I have found them to be very useful for me and helped awaken me to the inner aspect of certain exercises. They were especially unique in the explanation of the chakras or "centers" or "vortexes" in man and the different speeds or rates of vibration at which they operate. Understanding the centers is a central theme in this book. These Rites can now be found on the internet, and even some "groups" of spiritual nature have sprung up with these Rites at their core. I offer them up to you as a way to bring yourself up to the level necessary to practice martial art at your senior age. I would recommend you getting this book and reading it again and again, for some of the principles in this book will open you up to the spiritual origin of martial art.

Peter Kelder claimed that constant practice of these Rites shed the effects of years off his life and gave him youthful health throughout the remainder of his days. These Rites also developed certain "inner organs" that are necessary for the maintenance of health, and spiritual qualities not normally developed in ordinary life.

For me, these Rites have been a resource of rehabilitation from serious injury and disease. They also helped me emerge from very low states of physical, emotional and mental health. Although I have meant to do these for the rest of my life, I have been unable to persevere with them. However, each time the need arose and my pilot light was extinguished, they have brought me back from the dead.

From my medical background, I have realized that, in addition to strengthening the back and abdomen, these Rites also cause tonic stimulation of all the internal organs. This is because the nerves of the spine innervate every internal organ. When the spine becomes weak and inflexible, all kinds of disease states begin to manifest themselves in your life. Therefore I say to you, open your eye of revelation and light your pilot light with these Rites.

Rite One

Stand where you have plenty of open space in a room, dojang or outside. Hold both arms horizontally outstretched. Your right palm should face upward as if it was holding something. Left palm should be facing down. Spin to your right, clockwise. Begin slowly and pick up speed as much as is comfortable. If you become dizzy, stop. Spin as long as you desire. Sometimes in the beginning, you may become dizzy or disoriented when you stop. Make sure you have plenty of room. After doing this Rite many times, you will begin to notice that your mind will shut down, you will center in yourself and you will experience a sense of freedom.

Rite Two

Lie on your back with your arms at your side, palms down, and your legs together. While keeping your legs straight and knees locked out, lift them and your head and upper torso simultaneously, keeping toes pointed. Exhale while you are doing this. Fold your body together as far as it will go, chin resting on your chest. Hold this position for one count. Then relax the legs and torso simultaneously to the floor while inhaling. Repeat.

Rite Three

Kneel with both knees on the floor. Keep your pelvis and back straight, head erect and arms at your side. The toes may be pointed straight or bent back with the balls of the feet touching the ground. Bend forward while keeping your back straight and lower your chin to your chest. Exhale through the mouth as you do this. Keeping your hands at your sides, bend as far forward as is comfortable until you are about to lose your balance. Hold for one count. Then bend your torso backward and lay your head back as far as it will go so that it rests on your shoulders. Bend as far back as you can while keeping the pelvis upright. Let your arms dangle backward and your head relax as if you were looking behind you. This will accentuate the arch. Inhale through this movement. Hold this position for one count. Repeat.

Rite Four

Sit on the floor with your legs straight and feet flexed toward the head. Place your hands, palms open, on the floor on each side of your pelvis. Lift your pelvis upward while bending your knees until you attain the posture called the "wrestler's bridge." Allow your head to lean backward as if you were trying to see the floor. Your torso and back should be parallel to the ground or slightly arched upward like trying to touch the ceiling with your navel. Inhale as you are performing this motion. Hold the apex of this posture for one count. Then lower the torso and return to the original sitting position. Bend your toes backward as far as they will go and bend your head forward to touch your chin to your chest. Exhale on this return movement. Hold this posture for one count. Repeat.

Rite Five

Kneel on the floor with your hands, knees and toes touching the floor (dog posture). Then lift your pelvis vertically so your buttocks, arms and legs form a tent or pyramid posture. Bend your head underneath as far as possible. Keep your arms and legs straight and try to touch your chin to your chest as if you were trying to see through your legs. Push your heels down as far down as possible while pressing the shoulders down and buttocks up. Exhale while performing this motion. Hold the apex of this posture for one count (downward dog). Then, in one motion, lower your torso and allow your stomach to lower toward the ground until the back is arched to the maximum and the arms are straight. Do not let your stomach or thighs touch the ground. Bend your head backward as if you were trying to see your heels. Inhale when performing this motion. Hold the highpoint of this posture for one count (upward dog). Repeat. You may have to experiment to find the optimal distance between your hands and feet. Ideally, you should not have to change this distance while performing the movement. Also, there should not be excessive strain on your back in either the "swayback" or "tent" posture.

Repetitions

Do these Rites each morning after waking up, but before breakfast. Begin by doing three repetitions for each Rite once daily for seven days. The second week, increase the repetitions by two, so that you will be doing five repetitions once daily. Continue to increase the number of repetitions by two each week until you have reached twenty-one repetitions for each Rite once daily. It will take ten weeks. Remember the forty day rule? The maximum benefit for these Rites come after the tenth week. After the tenth week, your abdomen and back will be strengthened to the point that you should be able to perform all taekwondo moves without straining your back. If you experience back pain while doing these Rites, or if you have back pain that is not alleviated by these Rites, *do not do them.* If this is the case, I do not recommend taekwondo for you. You could hurt yourself further.

If you cannot perform them, do not despair. If you cannot obtain the proper posture for each or all of the Rites, like the wrestler's bridge, just do what you can. You will improve. Remember that you are probably at a very low level of physical capability. If you can do only seven repetitions or fourteen repetitions comfortably, then do that. On the other hand, this means that your potential for physical development is great. Persevere, do not give up, remember your aim. Strive to raise your level of being.

Give it forty days. If you can do that, go on to the next chapter.

Rite 1

Stand straight with feet together and arms horizontal out to the side. The right palm should be up and the left palm facing down. Gradually start spinning, making sure you always turn clockwise (as if viewed from above). Do not fixate your eyes on anything. As you spin faster your legs will follow by themselves. It may take a while to figure out the footwork. If you get dizzy or off balance, simply stop. Be sure you have enough room to do this rotation without hitting furniture or walls. As you get more familiar with this technique, you can whirl faster or slower. When you become comfortable with this Rite, you will notice that your mind shuts down and the awareness of your self opens up. I have seen the Sufi Whirling Dervishes perform this Rite with a musical rhythm for an hour *with their eyes closed!* This rite is said to harmonize the three centers.

Rite 2

Lie flat on the floor with your hands by your side, palms down. Then, simultaneously lift your head and legs upward. Keep your legs together and straight, with knees locked. Exhale during this movement, and hold the pose for a moment at the top. Then, lower your head and legs to the ground at the same time and relax, while inhaling. Repeat the movement.

Rite 3

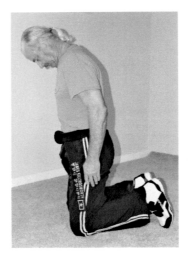

Kneel on the floor with your torso straight. Hold for a moment. Then, lean forward as far as you can without losing your balance. Bend your head forward on this movement and try to touch your chin to your chest. Exhale. Then lean backward as far as possible while keeping your thighs vertical. Inhale on this movement. Hold this posture for a moment, then repeat.

Rite 4

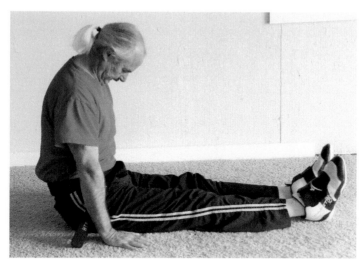

Begin by sitting on the floor with your legs straight and your palms on the ground. Your torso is vertical and your chin is on your chest. Push your hips forward and raise them vertically as far as you can go, and lean your head back like you're trying to look behind you. Inhale on this movement. Hold for a moment. Then, lower yourself to the ground gently to the original position. Exhale during this movement. Repeat.

Rite 5

Kneel on the ground in dog position, with your hands and knees on the floor. In one motion, lift your hips upward and point your buttocks to the sky. Push your shoulders backward to get maximum height. Point your face downward, so that you are looking between your legs (downward dog). You should sense a strain in your hamstrings. Exhale on this movement. Hold for a moment. Then, let your body drop easily into an upward dog. Your back should be arched and your head tilted back as if you are looking at the ceiling. Do not let your legs touch the floor. Inhale on this movement. Hold for a moment, then repeat the downward dog.

Chapter 2

As Above,
so Below.

Emerald Tablets of Hermes Trismegistus

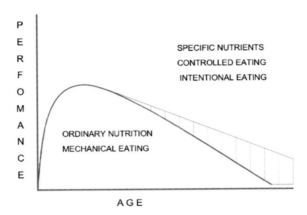

Nutritional Striving
for
Peak Performance

Nutrition

In 1983, I read a book called *Life Extension: A Practical Scientific Approach* by Durk Pearson and Sandy Shaw. Durk was a graduate student at MIT, and Sandy was at Berkley. Computers were mainly available at higher education institutions, and the internet was then in its infancy. Durk and Sandy used their computers to access nutritional studies, cataloged in libraries around the world. That information was distilled into this book. *Life Extension* is about three inches thick.

Although I am a pharmacist, pharmacy school was very disappointing for me, because it only emphasized synthetic drugs. Later, I understood the reason for this. The major drug companies had completed their stranglehold on our medical-pharmaceutical-industrial complex with their patented synthetic products. In fact, in 1973 I took the very last course in Pharmacognosy, the study of naturally derived pharmaceuticals.

Because I held degrees in biology and chemistry, in addition to pharmacy, my view of the human condition opened my eyes to disease, aging, suffering and death. This inclination was reinforced by the death of my father, a pediatrician, when he was sixty-three. I was only twenty. All of these factors nagged at me as if something was missing from my education. My experience told me something else was out there.

The moment I opened this book, *Life Extension*, I knew I had found what I was looking for. It showed me that nutrition played a major role in one's health and could improve its quality and possibly extend human life. This developed into a thirty-plus year practical study of nutrition.

When I began taekwondo in 1992 at the age of forty-four, the question of nutrition came to the forefront. How long could I practice taekwondo? Could nutrition improve my performance? Would nutrition extend my longevity in martial arts? Could nutrition even extend my life?

From a pharmacist's perspective, I am appalled at the average person's ignorance of nutrition. I am also simply horrified at the lack of understanding of nutrition in the medical establishment. In fact, in many cases it negates the role nutrition plays in preventative medicine and disease treatment. Back then, I found out that of the 109 medical schools in this country, only eight required any nutritional courses as part of their curriculum. I realized then I could not count on reliable information from doctors on this subject.

As a result of my studies and practical application of nutrition in my life, I have come to some definite conclusions about certain nutrients and their value in my training. I realize that I have a unique perspective on the subject because of the blending of my pharmaceutical and martial art practice.

It is my wish that this knowledge will be of benefit for your health in general. More specifically, I hope this knowledge will support your growth and development in martial art, and augment your ability to grow in your training.

Remember, nutrition and supplements are most valuable when your training brings you to the edge of your physical envelope.

Please consult your pharmacist or your doctor for any interactions that may exist between your prescription medication and nutrient supplementation. For more information about nutrients or references, go to *Life Extension Foundation-lef.org.*

The Control of the Inflammatory Response

Taekwondo is a very strenuous sport. The body operates at the edge of its physical envelope. As a result, the muscles, tendons, ligaments and joints must recover from the efforts of training. After each training session, a natural inflammatory process takes place. It is part of your healing and recovery. When you are young, the control of the inflammatory process is at its peak. Your recovery is as fast as possible and healing can be done overnight. As you get older, *all physiological, chemical and psychological processes slow down*. As a result, young people can train at the edge of their envelope almost every day and recover fast enough to continue this pace. Seniors however, like you and me, take longer to recover from the inflammatory process after hard training sessions.

Physiologically speaking, the rate of the chemical reactions that create energy, metabolize waste products and replenish nutrients are dependent on many factors. Some of these you can modify and some you cannot. We will be focusing your nutrition, which can definitely reduce the inflammatory process. Below are four main areas you can experiment with to modify the base level of inflammation in your body. There is a blood test that can measure this level. It is called *C-reactive protein*. Your doctor can order this test. It should be below 0.1.

1. Reduce your meat intake.

Meat is a highly inflammatory food. It contains large amounts of arachidonic acid. Arachidonic acid has a metabolic pathway of its own. It is metabolized into inflammatory prostaglandins that cause cell destruction, pain and swelling. These prostaglandins also depress your immune system. Plant-based diets reduce the inflammatory process and stimulate the immune system. If you cannot control your meat intake, you will needlessly suffer a great deal and seriously reduce the quality and longevity of your martial art career.

2. Reduce your Omega 6 and Omega 9 intake.

There are only three types of fats or oils. They are called Omega 6, 9 and 3. Omega 6's and 9's stimulate the inflammatory response and depress your immune system. They activate the same inflammatory prostaglandins that arachidonic acid does. Guess what? Omega 6's and 9's are mainly found in animal flesh, or anything with a face on it. Omega 3's however, reduce the inflammatory process and stimulate the immune system. Omega 3's are mostly found in deep water fish and certain plants like flax. Although the body needs all three fats, the ratio of 6's and 9's to the Omega 3's is twenty to one in the North American diet. It is this ratio that causes Americans to have the highest rates of hypertension, heart disease, diabetes and cancer in the world. The proper ratio is four to one. Omega 6's and 9's are found in all meats, especially beef. In addition, most oils, especially corn oil, peanut oil and other plant oils are almost all 6's and 9's. The *only* oil you should use for cooking is Extra Virgin Olive oil and for high heat cooking, Canola oil. These oils are "neutral oils", containing a balanced mixture of 3's, 6's and 9's. Unless you eat a mostly plant-based diet you should also take fish oil to increase your Omega 3 levels. The safest fish oil is *molecularly distilled fish oil,* which has absolutely no contaminates. Omega 3 fatty acids are special nutrients. We will talk more about them later.

3. Reduce your weight.

Fat is extremely inflammatory. Excess fat produces many inflammatory compounds. Fat also secretes estrogen. Estrogen produces metabolic products that are inflammatory. If your aim is to grow and maintain a high level of performance in martial art, you must seriously consider the burden that excess fat places on your joints, circulatory system, and every organ system of your physical body. If I placed a backpack on you that weighed 20, 30, 40 or more pounds, it would be very uncomfortable. You would immediately want to remove it because it interferes with your ability to move, and tires you quickly. This the same thing that extra weight does to you.

Why does this happen to almost all of us? There are many reasons, and you must understand and struggle with all of them to reach your proper weight. Here are some of them:

- We live in a culture where food is easy to come by and cheap.

- The foods that are easiest and cheapest to procure are the most caloric-dense and the most inflammatory.

- We are slaves to our sense organs, especially our sense of taste and smell, which are enhanced as we age.

- Our suggestibility is constantly bombarded by advertisements for food on TV.

- The food industry has created foods that taste better than unprocessed, natural foods.

- The average person is uneducated when it comes to nutrition and what the body really needs.

- We need to understand what type of influences we are under and how they affect our eating habits.

- We should have an aim or a goal that forces us to struggle with our weaknesses, including our eating habits.

- We must take responsibility for the preparation of our own food.

- We do not see that our body is a reflection of what we put into it.

4. Reduce sodium in your diet.

Sodium is of special importance in senior diets. If you are over 50 years old, you should not take in more than 1500mg of salt per day, about ½ teaspoonful. Seventy-five percent of the sodium in our diet comes from processed foods and fast foods. One *Hungry Man* frozen dinner has twice the amount of our recommended daily intake. Because excess sodium makes the body retain water, if you eat out a lot you probably have five to ten pounds of extra fluid in you. You also probably have high blood pressure. One single dinner at any restaurant can cause me to gain 3-4 pounds. Tap water and bottled water usually have a lot of dissolved salts in them (plus pesticides and micro plastics). Prepare and drink your beverages (coffee, tea etc.) only with distilled water or reverse osmosis water. Most people in the North American culture consume 3-4 times the recommended daily allowance of salt. Excess sodium increases your blood pressure, puts more strain on your heart and can damage your kidneys.

For me, my ring finger is a good barometer of excess sodium in my body. If my ring slides off easily then my sodium balance is good. If I have difficulty taking it off then there is swelling in my fingers which reflects too much sodium in my body. I have found that the only thing that reduces excess sodium in the body is sweating as a result of a good training session.

What Is Our Proper Weight?

There are many doctors that have practiced medicine all over the world. This group of doctors have found some interesting facts about the different cultures of the world and the relationship of their diet to their health. In cultures that do not have enough food to eat, they have very little fat on their bodies. They do not have the cultural diseases that plague industrialized nations like ours. They rarely have diabetes, high blood pressure, heart disease (atherosclerosis) or cancer. This is called a *sustenance diet*. It consists mostly of grains, legumes, vegetables, fruits and rarely meat. The key point is that they do not get to eat whenever and whatever they want. They spend much of their time during the day in food procurement and preparation. They have less than one inch of belly fat around their abdomen.

These doctors have developed a simple way to find *your ideal weight*, if you are interested preventing heart disease, high blood pressure, diabetes and cancer. It is also important to you, as a senior martial art competitor, to reduce your weight to achieve maximum performance.

Men: For a height measurement of five feet (60 inches), begin with 100 pounds. For each additional inch over five feet, add 5 pounds. For example, a six-foot man would be 100 pounds, plus 12 inches multiplied by 5 pounds (60 pounds), so his ideal weight is 160 pounds.

Women: For a height measurement of five feet, begin with 90 pounds. For each additional inch over five feet, add 4 pounds. For example, a five-foot-seven inch woman would be 90 pounds, plus 7 inches multiplied by 4 pounds (28 pounds), so her ideal weight is 118 pounds.

You must realize there are cultural differences for weight, especially in countries like ours where there is so much food. Over past decades, babies' birth-weights are increasing, children are growing faster and taller, and adult size and weights have been on the rise. Also, understand that our culture is in an obesity crisis.

I know what you are thinking or perhaps even saying out loud with an exclamation mark. "That weight is impossible for me!" Remember what this book is about. You want to participate and excel in martial art over 50, 60 or even 70 years or more. Do not forget your aim. See if what I say is true for you. I am giving you the ideal. Strive for the ideal and raise your level of being. Always consult a doctor before you try to change your diet or lose weight.

In trying to get down to my ideal weight, 160 pounds, I had to struggle a great deal and give up a lot (conscious suffering). The greatest sacrifice has been my ignorance and stupidity about my diet and my ego. The closest I could get was within five pounds. I could maintain 170-175 pounds comfortably. I know that it is possible, for at the worst point of my life (physically speaking) I was pushing 200 pounds and struggling with martial art and my health.

If you want more reinforcement, look around at *the really good martial artists*, no matter what their age. Rarely will you find one that is overweight. What you will find are many that are thin, wiry, flexible, and strike like a bull whip.

Caloric Restriction

If you are still skeptical about the role that excess weight plays in the destruction of your health, your physical potential and your longevity in martial arts, then listen to science. Caloric restriction is the *only proven activity that will prolong life.* Ponder a great deal about that. If it will prolong life, it will also prolong your life in martial art.

There are six major ways to restrict calories.

1. Reduce caloric-dense foods. Caloric-dense foods are meats, dairy products, fatty products (meats and oils) and sugar products (refined carbohydrates). Caloric-light foods are fruits, vegetables and legumes.

2. Skip one or more meals a day. I found that if I did not eat breakfast, I lost ten pounds in six weeks. That meant that the kind of breakfast I

was eating maintained ten pounds of my body weight. I felt great and gained back all the time spent in preparation, eating and cleaning up. It supported my resolve to control my cravings and helped me gain more power over the desires of my body.

3. Eat smaller portions.

4. Eat only within an eight-hour window. If you eat meals and snacks all through the day and night, your internal organs do not function as they should. Instead of being active players in your metabolism, they simply become passive. They become like slaves to the constant, unpredictable and irrational ingestion of all kinds of food at all different times. The desires of the organs of taste and smell become the active force of your metabolism. The liver, digestive system and pancreas do not have time to rest, and cannot send all of the nutrients down their correct metabolic pathways. It is like a metabolic traffic jam. They become weak and unresponsive like the rest of the body. If you fast for at least twelve to sixteen hours every day, the internal organs become true regulators of health. They harmonize with each other and interact in the most efficient manner. As a result of this harmony, you feel better, have less need for food and have real control over your eating habits. It has been shown that this window of nutrition practice will produce a ten percent reduction in weight. If you wish to excel in martial art, you need to try this practice.

5. Detoxing. Every once in a while my wife and I do a ten-day detox. Dr. Mark Hyman's book, *10-Day Detox Diet* is what we follow. We give up sugar (all refined carbohydrates), alcohol, caffeine, fried foods and dairy products. All we eat is fish, nuts, fruits and vegetables. The first few days result in suffering, because you are basically withdrawing from your food addiction. However, after the fourth day, your body begins to harmonize and *you feel great*. We usually lose around eight pounds after two weeks. After that time, you may add back some of these foods, or like us, do not add back some of the foods and permanently restrict them from your diet. For me, the major benefit from this detox *is that you have psychological control over your eating habits now, and have aligned your diet with your aim in martial art!*

Remember, it can take up to forty days of struggle to weaken your specific desires, cravings and mechanical behavior related to food.

6. Try to sense your desires or cravings when they arise, and know that you could resist the temptation to indulge in them. Below are the cravings in me that I know very well, and they inhabit all human beings.

   A) Sugar craving.

   B) Meat craving.

   C) Fat craving.

   D) Salt craving.

   E) Sugar/fat craving.

   F) Sugar/fat/salt craving.

   G) I am not full craving.

   Look on your plate and it will be a reflection of your food desires or cravings. Know if you are really hungry or is it a craving.

   These are your nutritional enemies.

The Role of Specific Nutrients

Specific nutrients can be helpful in health, but without acting on the previous major caveats mentioned, they are just a minor side-show. However, if you can act on these caveats, then specific nutrients can perfect your striving, *especially if your training pushes you to the edge of your physical envelope.* Let us look at some important ones.

Nutrients to Control the Inflammatory Response

Curcumin

Curcumin is a substance found in the spice turmeric, which is a member of the ginger family. Turmeric is a traditional spice used liberally in India. Curcumin has been extensively studied in animals, where it has demonstrated anti-cancer and anti-arthritic activity. In addition, these studies show that curcumin is a strong antioxidant and protects against amyloid formation in the brain that leads to Alzheimer's disease. Curcumin protects the arteries from lipid peroxidation (rancidity) that leads to atherosclerosis (an inflammatory process of the arteries) and prevents blood clots by inhibiting platelet aggregation (the beginning of clotting process). Protection of your arterial walls is of paramount importance to the maintenance of a healthy circulatory system. I have taken it for over five years and feel it really reduces soreness after workouts and contributes to my low C-Reactive-Protein Test (a measure of overall inflammation). The usual dosage is 400 mg twice daily. Be sure to find a product with good bioavailability, for curcumin is not very well absorbed.

Omega 3 Fatty Acids

Earlier, we talked about the detriment of too much Omega 6 and Omega 9's in your diet. Conversely, Omega 3's *are good for you*! Unless you have a plant based diet and eat fatty, deep water fish three times a week, you need to supplement with Omega 3 fatty acids. The only reliable source of Omega 3 fatty acids is fish oil. It does not need to be modified or acted on by the body to do its work. *It depresses inflammation and stimulates your immune system.* The discovery of the benefits of Omega 3 fatty acids is one of the great advances of health science in my opinion. For you as a martial artist with strenuous training bouts, this is one of the best protective nutrients you can take to reduce inflammation caused by training. If you eat mostly a plant-based diet, take one or two grams per day. If you eat a meat-based diet (four or more times per week), take four grams per day. The big caveat with fish oil is its purity. Most fish oil comes from farm-raised Atlantic salmon, which are fed ground up little fish. These little fish concentrate all of the pollutants that plague our oceans into the farm-raised salmon. Imagine that one little fish has one unit of toxin in it. If a big fish eats one hundred little fish, then it concentrates by one hundred times this toxin in the tissue of the big fish. Very toxic methyl mercury, PCP's (poly-chlorinated phenols) and endocrine disrupters (pesticides, plastics and herbicides) are in normal processed fish oil. The only safe fish oil is *molecularly distilled* fish oil. This type of fish oil is highly purified and has no contaminates in it.

Protect and Improve your Circulation

Your circulatory system is one of the most important aspects of the aging process, and needs to be developed and protected to the highest degree possible. Martial art exercise is one of the best physical training programs to develop the heart and blood vessels. Martial art exercises *all* the muscles of the body and therefore improves the circulation to all body parts. All out sparring, forms practice and drills create bursts of activity requiring balance, speed, power and endurance.

Inside the heart and arteries there is a single layer of specialized cells called the *endothelium*. The endothelial cells line the inner part of these vessels. These cells produce nitrous oxide that causes the arteries to dilate, increase blood flow and lower blood pressure. If you opened all of the arterial walls and laid them out flat on the ground, the average male would have a square area equal to about six tennis courts. As we age, the endothelial cells become damaged due to our diet, inflammation, smoking, alcohol, diabetes and other disease states. As the square area of the endothelium decreases, the systolic blood pressure gradually increases because the arteries lose their elasticity. Remember that the elasticity depends on nitrous oxide production. The development of high blood pressure, atherosclerosis and plaque formation are in direct relationship with the loss of the endothelium. It is important that you read and understand the previous discussion about inflammation, because it is the same process that is happening in your arteries and is destroying your endothelium. In severe cases of heart disease (atherosclerosis) or diabetes, the endothelium is so damaged that you may only have one and one-half tennis courts of healthy endothelium! Once endothelial cells are destroyed, they cannot be replaced. If you wish to have a future in martial arts, or indeed *a future at all*, you must protect your circulatory system and the endothelium. Let us explore what can be done to preserve your circulatory system and reduce the inflammatory process.

1. Do not smoke. It destroys your endothelium.

2. Reduce meat intake in your diet. Reread the part in this chapter on inflammation. Animal-based diets increase the inflammatory process that destroys endothelial cells.

3. Avoid refined sugar and high fructose corn syrup. These are two of the most deadly substances you can take into your body. They are in almost every processed food. Nearly anything in a box, can or package

has these in them. They are converted instantly into glucose and drive your glucose levels up dramatically. Excess circulating glucose combines with proteins in the blood. These are called glycoproteins. They are very stable and remain in the blood for months. These glycoproteins are very damaging to the endothelium. They act like tiny bits of sand moving through your circulatory system. The effect is like rubbing sand paper on your skin. It damages your skin, and causes redness, swelling and pain. Surgeons who perform heart bypass operations report that the inside of the damaged arteries are bright red and extremely inflamed. The measure for the concentration of these glycoproteins is called A1C. It shows the relative amount of sugar taken into your body over the last six months. You want an A1C level of less than six, but preferably less than five. Any level above seven makes you a diabetic. Levels greater than eight will cause definitive damage to your circulatory system. You may experience poor circulation in your extremities, eyes and internal organs. The lack of circulation will lead to nerve damage and symptoms of diabetic neuropathy - absence of sensation or "pins and needles pain." If you want to have longevity in martial arts over fifty, avoid refined sugar and high fructose corn syrup.

4. Train anaerobically. Any exercise is good for you. Martial art requires extreme exertion over relatively short periods of time with short rests in between, at least for tournament competition. Much of your activity will be in anaerobic mode, meaning that you do not have enough breath. You should train for this. When you do form, sparring, weapons or plyometric training, continue to train for forty to sixty minutes, but never quite regain your breath until the end of the workout. This is the best training you can do for your circulatory system.

Nutrients That Protect and Improve Circulation

Pomegranate

Pomegranate is the source of powerful antioxidants called "punicalagins." These have been shown to have many medical benefits. Pomegranate promotes wound healing and reduces the inflammatory process. The most important benefit is that it protects the endothelium and improves arterial blood flow. Studies have shown that if the extract is taken regularly for one to two years it *improves arteriole blood flow by 30%*! Stay away from the juice that is high in sugar and low in concentration. Take only the extract.

Superoxide Dismutase (SOD)

The physical body is an energy factory. It takes in solid and liquid food and combines it with oxygen to create a burning process (oxidation) that produces the energy that we sense and use as a living creature. This is called metabolism and it occurs in each cell of the body. It is like a controlled burn. On a cellular level, some of the byproducts of this metabolism are free radicals. These are atoms that are missing electrons on their outer orbits (oxidants). They are electron-hungry, so to speak. In their search for electrons they do not care where they get the electrons needed and attack healthy cells. Free radicals are destructive to cells if not neutralized by substances called *antioxidants* that donate electrons. Many of the foods we eat, especially fruits and vegetables, have antioxidants in them, and are very beneficial in protecting us from free radicals. However, the body produces two powerful antioxidants that protect us from our own metabolism. Without these two endogenous antioxidants we would literally burn up or fry. One is called glutathione and the other is superoxide dismutase (SOD). Glutathione is especially protective for your liver. In fact, glutathione is destroyed by the drug acetaminophen. Acetaminophen poisoning is the number one cause of liver failure in this country, and is responsible for about 40,000 deaths each year. Take too much acetaminophen and your liver literally fries. NAC (N-acetyl-cysteine) is the precursor to glutathione and is given in cases of acetaminophen poisoning. While glutathione protects the liver, SOD safeguards your endothelium. SOD protects the lining of the arteries. As you age, your body produces less SOD (like everything else) so you want to increase these levels. One way to help is to eat plenty of spinach. Yes, Popeye had it right. Spinach has been proven to increase SOD levels. Much of SOD is destroyed in your stomach if taken orally. Up until recently, no oral formulations were available for supplementation. Now there is a stable oral formulation of SOD combined with pomegranate extract. It is the best of both worlds. I really recommend you take this formulation. It is called *Endothelial Defense*, sold by Life Extension.

Quercetin

Quercetin is a unique bioflavonoid found in red wine, black and green tea, red onions, red grapes, tomatoes, broccoli, cherries and raspberries. Bioflavonoids are compounds that are found in plants and fruits that have nutritional and medicinal properties in animals and human beings. Many bioflavonoids have distinctive colors. Quercetin has potent anti-inflammatory and anti-allergy effects. It is useful in allergies and allergy related diseases like asthma and bronchitis. It also lowers C-reactive protein (a measure of the body's overall inflammatory state). High levels of C-reactive protein are associated with a gamut of disease states, including obesity, heart disease and lupus. For me the most interesting function of quercetin is that it stabilizes capillary fragility. This means that it strengthens small blood vessels and improves circulation. It is used to reduce bleeding and prevent bruising. For years, I have recommended quercetin to seniors who suffer from ecchymosis (subcutaneous bruising). If you are a senior martial artist, you should take this supplement to protect your circulatory system. The usual dosage is 250mg twice a day. Check with your doctor if you take this supplement while you are on blood thinners. In fact, if you are on blood thinners, I would not recommend you do martial art.

Coenzyme Q10

Coenzyme Q10, in my opinion, is one of the greatest nutritional discoveries in the last thirty years. Ubiquinone (its chemical name) is found in every cell of the body. It is an oil soluble, vitamin-like substance in the mitochondria (energy factories). It is a component of the electron transport chain and participates in aerobic cellular respiration, generating energy in the form of a molecule called ATP (adenosine triphosphate). Ninety-five percent of the human body's energy is generated in this way. Therefore, those organs with the highest energy requirements, such as the heart, liver and kidneys, have the highest Coenzyme Q10 levels. To protect your heart from the extreme energy demands placed on it by martial art is of primary concern, and supplementation with Coenzyme Q10 can be helpful in energy restoration. Ubiquinone, available in oral form, is not absorbed well with only about 40% absorption. Ubiquinol, the reduced form of ubiquinone, is 60 to 80% absorbed, and is the actual substance used in energy reactions. Later on we will talk more about this remarkable substance when we talk about energy restoration.

Nutrients for Energy Restoration

One of the most important ideas to get across to you, my senior reader, is that *all biochemical functions* decrease in rate as we age. (See the graph.) Even though we can train with young people, and hold our own, we just can't do it as long as they can. Nor can we recover from workouts as fast as they can. This is because the rate of energy recovery, chemically speaking, deteriorates with age. For example, young people can have hard training episodes nearly every day, because their energy recovery rate is in its prime. For you or me, however, it may take one or two days to recover fully from that same training episode. It is because the mitochondria (energy factories in each cell) cannot manufacture the chemicals fast enough to produce enough ATP (the energy molecule that allows us to expend energy). The chemical pathways and substrates (molecules needed to produce energy) in energy production have long been worked out and isolated. It is called the Kreb's cycle, or aerobic cellular respiration. Ninety-five percent of our energy comes from these chemical reactions. If we delve deeper into the atoms that compose the molecules in these reactions, we find something called an *electron transport chain*, which actually forms the ATP molecule. In studying these energy chemical reactions, it has been found that certain substances are of more value to the reactions than others. In other words, the concentrations of these substances are *the rate-limiting steps* in energy production. If their concentrations are depressed then the energy reactions slow down and the rate of energy restoration is impeded. You recover slower. It has been found that if you supplement with these certain substances, the ATP concentrations increase, and the rate of energy restoration increases. This is very valuable knowledge to you as a senior martial art practitioner. Let us examine some of these substances you may want to supplement with.

Ubiquinol

In the early 1950's, the drug company Merck isolated and patented a substance we now call Coenzyme Q10. They named it ubiquinone, meaning "everywhere." Indeed, it is in every cell of the body in the mitochondria, the energy factories of the cell. It is an important link in the electron transport chain that forms the high energy molecules called ATP. Merck did not know what they had and sold the patent to a Japanese company. If they hadn't, it would have probably become a prescription item, and we would have paid big bucks for it. Ubiquinone is reduced to the active form ubiquinol in the cell. When we age, as I have spoken about before, the production rates of all substances fall, including ubiquinol. It has been found that we can supplement with ubiquinol and increase our cellular levels, and therefore increase the rate at which our cells can produce energy. In fact, the concentrations of ubiquinol is a *rate-limiting step* in the production of energy. This is important to you, an aging martial art practitioner. There are a few things you need to know about supplementation. First, ubiquinone is cheap but it is only absorbed about forty percent if taken orally. Second, ubiquinone must be reduced (converted) into the active form *ubiquinol* before it can enter into the electron transport chain. Ubiquinol is absorbed eight times more than ubiquinone and does not need to be converted to be active. Studies have shown that supplementation with ubiquinol and two other nutrients, D-ribose and L-carnitine, have cut recovery time in half for heart attack patients! On the other hand, several prescription drugs depress ubiquinol levels, like statin drugs (cholesterol lowering agents) and beta blockers (blood pressure lowering agents). Statin drugs can reduce ubiquinol levels by forty percent! As a result, this can also cause a severe muscle disease called rhabdomyolysis. If you take statin drugs and have prolonged, unexplained muscle aches or weakness, call your doctor or pharmacist immediately.

D-Ribose

D-Ribose is a simple sugar found in the cells that is another important part of energy production. Depleted concentrations of D-Ribose in the mitochondria depress production of ATP. Studies have shown that D-Ribose supplementation rapidly restores cellular ATP levels.

L-Carnitine

L-Carnitine is a unique substance found in the mitochondria. Its function is to facilitate the use of fatty acids to produce energy. In addition to carbohydrate metabolism to produce energy, fatty acid metabolism is just as important to energy production. L-Carnitine can help restore energy after exercise to normal levels, therefore enhancing recovery after exercise. Acetyl-l-carnitine crosses the blood brain barrier, thereby reducing oxidative stress (imbalance of free radicals and antioxidants) and promoting energy production in the central nervous system. In addition, it supports the synthesis and release of dopamine and acetylcholine, which are important neurotransmitters. It also stimulates the production of nitrous oxide, the molecule that is responsible for dilatation of the blood vessels.

Dr. Stephen Sinatra and Dr. James Roberts, cardiac specialists, published a book called *Reverse Heart Disease Now*. These doctors also are athletes in their own right by being long distance cyclists and runners. By using integrative medicine with nutritional support they achieved remarkable recoveries in their cardiac patients with the use of ubiquinol, D-ribose and L-carnitine. Being athletes themselves, they realized the importance of these nutrients in sports recovery. You should read this book.

Nutrients to Improve Joint Health

Taekwondo can be the best thing for your flexibility and your joints, or it can be the worst thing. If you create and maintain a stretching program when you begin martial art, parallel to your taekwondo training, you will have the best of both worlds. If you do not, then I guarantee you will suffer a setback in the way of joint injury. The problem is that all techniques, especially kicking techniques, require twisting or torsional motion of your toes, ankles, knees, hips, back and shoulders. As you progress in your taekwondo journey, your joints will naturally become stronger and more flexible. But I can tell you that the rate of advancement will out-pace the preparedness of your joints, and you will begin to have injuries, some of them severe, that will retard or stop your training. When you begin jumping techniques, the likelihood of your landing incorrectly is elevated, and the possibility of a major injury skyrockets. I have had first-hand experience with joint injuries. For most martial art training, stretching is incidental.

Most of your instructors will be younger than you and will not understand your needs as a senior. Their priority is to guide you through their curriculum as if you were an average student. You are not. Time is also an issue for stretching. It takes time before and after class, and is a separate practice by itself. But if you understand the sense and significance of what I am now saying, and practice diligently, your rewards will be great, and your longevity in martial art will be impressive and admired. Stretching is so important that it has its own chapter in this book. Read it and understand it well. If you do, then the following nutritional points will enhance your joint health. If not, the nutrition supplementation will be of limited value. Three basic preventative measures are – reduce weight, eat a plant based diet and stretch your joints regularly.

Contemporary medical science views degenerative joint problems as a disease state. This is typical thinking because the drug companies have a "treatment" in the form of an expensive drug regimen. The usual treatment is pain drugs, anti-inflammatory drugs, steroids, injections and then surgery. These treatments are palliative, and over time these same drugs will actually deteriorate your cartilage. The average person has neglected their joint health by being overweight, eating an inflammatory diet and not recovering completely from an injury of some sort. Also, doing some type of repetitive stressful joint activity, usually associated with their job or lifestyle, deteriorates the joints.

Glucosamine Sulfate

In the ageing process the body's ability to produce substrates (food) for the chemical reactions that maintain the restorative process deteriorates. The disease called osteoarthritis (inflammation of the joints) is really a condition that is caused by the body's reduced ability to produce a substance called glucosamine. Glucosamine is a natural substance in the body that is the building block of the glycosaminoglycan. The glycosaminoglycan is a matrix of long chained molecules that form the sponge-like material in between our joints that we call cartilage. This cartilage holds a fluid called synovial fluid that cushions the impact on the ends of our bones as we push away from the earth with our muscles. Cells called chondrocytes are located on the end surface of each bone. These chondrocytes take glucosamine and produce the glycosaminoglycan that maintain the cartilage web.

As we age, our body does not produce enough glucosamine to maintain a healthy thickness of cartilage between the bones. As the cartilage thins out, it holds less synovial fluid. Less synovial fluid causes more stress on the joints. This condition is likened to a sponge losing water and drying out. As a result, we get inflammation, pain and swelling in our joints.

Fortunately, it has been found that if we supplement our diet with glucosamine, the chondrocytes will make new cartilage, maintain our joint health and prevent the onset of osteoarthritis. The difficulty comes from the fact that glucosamine is only found naturally in one thing - exoskeletons of shrimp. Of course, most of us probably do not eat that part of the shrimp. Glucosamine supplements are made from ground up shrimp tails. There are two other important aspects of supplementing with glucosamine. First it needs to be consumed as the glucosamine sulfate salt. Sulfur is a very important part of the cartilage chemical makeup. Second, find a supplement that also combines MSM with the glucosamine sulfate. Methyl sulfur methane sounds bad but in the chemical world it is called a "methyl donor." The chemical pathways that form cartilage require large amounts of methyl groups to form the branches of the cartilage. The proper daily dosage to maintain cartilage health is 1500 mg of glucosamine sulfate in divided doses (750 mg twice daily). If you are allergic to shrimp, there is a synthetic form available that you can take. Begin taking glucosamine sulfate in your late forties, or when you begin to experience any joint discomfort, and continue for the rest of your life. If your joints reach the point where the bones rub together (bone on bone), glucosamine supplementation will not help, because all of the chondrocytes that produce cartilage have been ground off.

In the original book, *The Arthritis Cure* by Jason Theodosakis, MD and Sheila Buff, another product called chondroitin was also touted for joint health. However, in my experience, all of the studies (hundreds of them) were done with glucosamine. Glucosamine has a 99% absorption rate and works. In addition, the origin of chondroitin is the desiccated, ground up nasal septum of calves that have been slaughtered. Chondroitin is a large molecule made of many amino acids. It is broken down into its component parts during digestion, and there is no evidence that it makes it to the chondrocytes. It makes the formulation more expensive. It is another cow byproduct.

To prevent joint problems, you should begin taking glucosamine sulfate when you begin martial art, and take it for the rest of your life.

Muscle Soreness

Muscle soreness is part of training. When you train hard, the exercise causes a systemic inflammatory response in the muscles, joints and connective tissue that were put under stress. It can be thought of as the results of your training, when it is strenuous enough to cross the edge of your previous physical envelope. It can also be thought of as a triad. The active force is your training, the retarding force is your soreness, and the recovery process is your neutralizing or equilibrating force. For me, soreness was actually something of a gauge of my physical envelope and how good a training session I had. I would try to train hard enough in the morning to begin to experience soreness two to three hours after stopping. Usually, it was mild or moderate discomfort that would continue the rest of the day, but not enough to keep me from sleeping through the night. The next morning, the soreness would nearly be gone or continue in the form of a mild sense of the discomfort. Mild to moderate soreness is a good indication that you are training enough to grow in your ability. Such soreness was always gone by the end of the second day, so that on the third day I could train all over again. I actually came to enjoy the soreness, as it enhanced the sense of my body existing. The sense of your body existing is a most important subject. It will be explored again and again. See the chapter called The Organ of Sense. However, if my training produced a severe soreness, enough to interfere with my ordinary life, prevent me from sleeping, produce pain or last more than two days, then that was too much and indicated muscle or joint damage. Then I would rest a whole week before I trained again. This kind of soreness was usually produced when I went to a national training session, where we trained up to eight hours a day for one or more days. This training was particularly hard on us seniors, because the trainers were usually much younger than us, and of course, ninety percent of the students were young people. The other circumstance that produced severe soreness was a hard training session after a long layoff. As a pharmacist, working full time, I would have to stand on my feet ten hours every day. If my soreness was severe, I really suffered.

Naturally, most people do not understand soreness or its role in their training, so they self-medicate with over-the-counter pain medications like ibuprofen and naproxen. Several men I competed with would take ibuprofen before their workouts to prevent soreness or to reduce the pain they already had from some previous injury. Being a pharmacist, I warned them that these drugs would *mask the pain and could lead to overtraining and injury.* Not only that, these drugs may cause the stomach to bleed each time you take them and may also lead to kidney problems if taken over long periods.

Tart Cherry Extract

My experience with soreness and nutrition led me to take Tart Cherry Extract. This stuff really works. If I trained too hard and got moderate to severe soreness, I would take this natural product and it worked well. It is well-known for muscle restoration and recovery. It comes as a 480mg capsule and I would take one capsule twice daily after training. The soreness would be almost totally mitigated. I would recommend you to try this before you take synthetic drugs. *Remember, the soreness is just masked by the extract until it subsides. It does not make the physiological processes of soreness stop. You still have to rest until the soreness naturally subsides.*

Cramping

Sweating is part of training. It cools the body by evaporation. In so doing, sweating causes the loss of electrolytes like sodium, potassium and magnesium. These are found in your sweat. The most noticeable is sodium, which causes your sweat to taste salty. Magnesium is also an extremely important electrolyte in your sweat.

Magnesium

Over 300 different functions have been found in the body in which magnesium is a participant. It is one of the most important minerals in the body. It is necessary in proper heart, kidney, and muscle function. While our muscles need calcium to contract, *they need magnesium to relax.* Magnesium is sometime called the "relaxation mineral." In my practice in pharmacy, every spring, seniors come to me complaining of cramping in their legs or back. As a result of my detailed questioning, I would almost always find that the previous day they had spent digging in the dirt, preparing their garden or flower beds. This work caused them to sweat a lot. The sweating, combined with the un-accustomed work, would invariably produce cramping. Sometimes it was so severe they could not sleep. I would recommend a long-acting magnesium chloride and they would be relieved within a day. I extended this knowledge to my martial art training, and while consuming this mineral I was usually cramp free.

Magnesium comes in three major forms – magnesium oxide, magnesium citrate and magnesium chloride. Magnesium oxide, brand name *Mag Ox*, is a short-acting dosage form and must be taken three times daily. This results in the unpleasant side effect of diarrhea. Remember *Milk of Magnesia*? It is used to treat constipation, as is magnesium citrate. However there is a long-acting form of magnesium chloride that provides elemental magnesium without the side effect of diarrhea. This is what I recommend to prevent cramping and have used personally throughout my taekwondo career. One tablet twice daily would protect me from cramping and muscle soreness resulting from hard, sweaty training sessions. The brand name is called *Mag 64* and there are generics available.

Nutritionally speaking, magnesium is found in abundance in fruits and vegetables. Dark leafy greens, nuts and seeds, soy beans, avocados, bananas, dark chocolate, yogurt and fish are the top dietary sources for magnesium. It has been found that even eating a plant-based diet may not provide enough magnesium, due to our soils being depleted of the mineral through intensive farming practices. For this reason, it has been said that five out of every seven people may be deficient in magnesium. Even testing the blood levels do not properly reflect the magnesium concentrations in the cells, so one could be deficient while having normal blood levels.

Some Closing Thoughts

It is important for you to realize that our bodies are a product of Mother Nature. The food we eat has been around since man has existed. Excluding meat, all the fruits and vegetables not only give us nourishment but also have become symbiotic with the human body. Each fruit and vegetable contains *phytonutrients* that protect us from the process of living. The process of living is the cellular process of energy production, or controlled oxidation. The oxidative process produces metabolic products that can damage our bodies called free radicals. Fruits and vegetables contain important antioxidants that protect us from these free radicals. It is interesting and unique to note that the colors of the fruits and vegetables reflect nutrients that protect specific organ systems in the body. When we ingest these colored fruits and vegetables, each colored nutrient goes to a specific place in the body or performs a specific function that protects that aspect of the body. The red colors protect the sex organs. For instance the reds in tomatoes, cherries and raspberries protect the prostate gland in males. The orange colors in peppers and carrots protect the lining of the lungs, abdomen and skin. The yellows of peppers, squash and corn protect the retina of the eye from ultraviolet radiation. The greens in spinach, cabbage, broccoli and peppers give us minerals (sodium, potassium and magnesium) that are needed to sustain electrolyte function in the blood and catalyze hundreds of intracellular reactions. In addition, spinach stimulates the production of the body's natural antioxidant SOD and broccoli shifts the metabolic toxins from hormone metabolism that cause cancer into harmless metabolic products. The blues and purples in grapes, wine and blueberries are some of the strongest antioxidants of the plant world. It is wise to eat fruits and vegetables of all colors. Meat has no phytonutrients.

A very important acronym for you to remember is called G-BOMBS. This term comes from a book titled *Eat to Live* by Dr. Joel Fuhrman. It means greens, beans, onions, mushrooms, berries and seeds. These foods provide specific substrates that are important for a healthy intestinal biome. A healthy intestinal biome (flora or microorganisms) is critical to your health overall. Try to keep G-BOMBS in your diet on a regular basis. I highly recommend reading this book. It is the best treatise on nutrition I have ever read. I could find nothing in this book that was untrue.

Although this chapter deals with solid and liquid food, there are two other foods that human beings extract from the external world. Air is the second food. You can exist for sixty days without solid and liquid food, but you cannot live for five minutes without air. Impressions are the third food that supports the existence of the human being. You can only live for five minutes without air, but you cannot live for even a moment without impressions. Impressions are the food that maintains your five senses, your consciousness and the sense of yourself existing. Impressions come from influences that are higher than your consciousness. The study of the influences you are under is of paramount importance if you want to understand your *inner life.*

Chapter 3

*Flexibility in the body
reflects an openness
of the mind.*

FLEXIBILITY AND STRETCHING

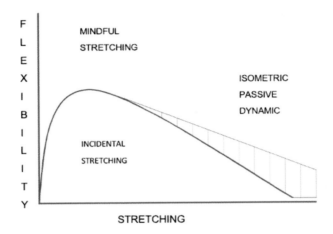

Flexibility and Stretching

Strength is the first level of your foundation in taekwondo, and flexibility is the second. During my experience in martial art, flexibility was neglected or mostly ignored. As a result, I suffered many injuries that I found out later I could have avoided if I had practiced a stretching regimen parallel to my taekwondo training. Yes, you will gradually become more flexible as you train, but in order to progress fully, with good quality technique and minimal injury, your flexibility training must be parallel or slightly ahead of class training.

I began taekwondo when I was forty-four. During my journey to purple belt, I was a basket case. I doubted my ability to continue because my flexibility stunk. I could not even put my foot on the kitchen counter. I had several muscle pulls, strains and severe soreness after class. Generally speaking, I was almost twenty years older than most students, and also my instructor. Therefore, they did not understand or address my lack of flexibility. This is still a common problem.

In class, performing the regular "warm up" used by young people, I never seemed to get stretched out, and my workouts suffered by not being able to perform the techniques throughout my full range of motion. By the time I did get warmed up, class was almost over. Our typical warm up consisted of jumping jacks or running in place, then punching or blocking drills. After that, we did straight leg raises, knee strikes and maybe some kicks. Then we would do passive stretching on the floor, like runner's stretches, frogs or splits. Finally, class would begin. It seemed fine for the youngsters, for they needed very little warm up, and many were blessed with natural flexibility, especially the ladies. Unfortunately, it did not meet my needs.

Frustrated by this situation, I began to read books on flexibility and stretching, and realized the spectrum of stretching was very wide and very sports-specific. I found that stretching is divided into five categories, and involves different techniques for each category. As a result of my studies, I decided there were only three types of stretching that would benefit my taekwondo training. They are dynamic, isometric and passive stretching. I found that dynamic stretching had all of the qualities that I needed to warm up and stretch out before class participation. I experimented and created my own warm up that was about five minutes in length. Most of the motions were similar to those used in my actual training. I performed it before each class, and was able to enter the class and perform on an equal level to the younger people. My goal was to be panting and sweating at the end of those five minutes.

Dynamic Stretching

Dynamic stretching is also called stretching through movement. Dynamic stretching produces three fundamental changes in the muscles, joints and circulatory system. First, like all other methods, it stretches the length of the muscle. Second, it increases circulation, causing muscle temperature to rise. This is consistent with the type of training you will be participating in. A warm muscle is twenty percent more flexible, twenty percent faster and twenty percent stronger than a cold muscle. Increased circulation leads to an increased metabolism that signals the body to activate the three energy storage systems - phosphagen, glycolysis and aerobic. A warm muscle allows more control over movement, especially complicated or precise ones. Proprioception is enhanced and reaction time is reduced. Third, dynamic stretching "resets" the resting length of the muscles, which allows for maximum range of motion in the shortest period of time. Dynamic stretching is the fastest way to achieve these three benefits. In five minutes, maximal flexibility and readiness can be achieved.

Sports-Specific Stretching

The human body is a unique and unbelievably adaptive organism. It can run over twenty miles without stopping, climb twenty-six thousand feet into the atmosphere and dive three hundred feet below the ocean. It can bludgeon itself against others for an hour, run as fast as twenty-five miles an hour, swim for days and leap over seven feet in the air. However, for each of these feats, the body must be prepared by training for each specific task. The first requirement of training is to stretch the muscles to the proper length and strength for the specific task.

Taekwondo is unique in that it requires maximum flexibility and strength in each joint simultaneously to perform the blocks, punches, kicks, jumps and spins in a seamless, integrated flow. Therefore, warming and stretching each joint is paramount to the proper execution in taekwondo training. Dynamic stretching prepares each joint for the upcoming strenuous activity in the shortest amount of time. In other words, you do not prepare for taekwondo by passive stretching. You warm up, stretch and prepare by performing the very same strikes and kicks that you will be doing in the training that follows.

Here is my warm up. It was developed to bring my *whole body* into a state of readiness, so that I could plunge into any endeavor with one hundred percent of my capability without fear of damaging my body. Perform these dynamic stretches every morning before engaging in your day and before each training session or competition event. It will raise your level of being.

Dynamic Warm Up

Upper Body

1. Neck rotations through entire range of motion. Ten repetitions each.

Front and back.

Side to side.

Over and back.

360-degree rotations left and right. (Do slowly and for only five repetitions).

2. Shoulder rotations through entire range of motion. Ten repetitions of each.

Bent arm swings. Exaggerate for maximum rotation.

Pec decks.

Windmills, forward and backward. Relax arms, allowing movement at shoulders only.

Sky waves. Do not lean forward; look up at the sky and bend at your waist to the side. These stretch the oblique muscles.

3. Back or trunk rotations. Twenty repetitions on each side.

Stand with a mirror in behind you. Rotate and make eye contact with yourself on each repetition. Try to practice a deep middle stance when doing these. Keep your trunk straight. You may increase the stretch by adding double outer forearm blocks or back fists on each rotation. The back usually takes double the amount of repetitions to stretch out. Do not skimp.

Lower Body

4. Butt kicks. Twenty repetitions on each side. Guard up.

Assume a cat stance. Try to actually kick yourself in the butt with your heel. Make the kicks pop you're uniform. This is great to warm up your knees.

5. Knee strikes. Ten repetitions on each side. Guard up.

Try to knee yourself in the chest, quickly.

6. Straight leg raises. Ten repetitions on each leg.

> This can be a leg swing at first. For more difficulty, assume a ready stance. Do not swing your leg; lift it quickly from full stop. Hold your hand high in front and touch it. This will strengthen the hip muscles and develop fast-twitch muscle fibers.

7. Outer crescent kicks. Ten repetitions on each leg.

> Accentuate hip rotation. For more difficulty, hold your hand out to the side and slap it with your foot.

8. Side kick chambers. Ten repetitions of each.

> Guard up, turn your head to look at the target, plant heel pointed at the target, chamber the knee in front of your body and hold it until your balance is achieved. Do this quickly, as if someone is rushing you.

9. Side kick straight leg swings for maximum height. Start with your side toward the target and lift your leg as high as possible. Ten repetitions on each leg.

> Lightly balance with your hand on the wall or chair and keep your lead hand behind your back. Try for maximum height and quickness.

10. Leg spreads on floor while lying on your back. Support your lower back if necessary. Twenty repetitions to begin with, and work up to one hundred.

11. Hamstring curls. Work yourself up to one hundred on each leg.

> Lie on a bed or bench face down with your knee just off the end. Do single hamstring curls. Start with twenty repetitions, half with ankle curled backward, heel up, and then the other half with ankle and toes extended in a front kick extension. This works different musculature around your knee.

Note that 10 and 11 are usually done at home.

Do these dynamic stretches four to five times a week. Make them the first thing you do in the morning after you wake up, before breakfast. Start slow at first and build up. In a week or two, you will notice that you are wide awake and ready for the day. In four to six weeks, you will be *able to kick a foot higher*. You will also notice that there is a certain residual flexibility that will stay with you all day. Develop your own routine to target your specific weaknesses or needs. Do these dynamic stretches before class and before going into the ring. You will soon begin to understand about *levels of being*, and what a higher level of being can mean for your life and your aim in martial art. Then you will start to look forward to the next level. Life will open up for you.

Passive Stretching

Sometimes called relaxed stretching, passive stretching is necessary to actually lengthen the muscles, tendons and ligaments over time.

There are three phases in developing your envelope of flexibility. The first phase is to "reset the resting length of the muscles." Dynamic stretching is the best and quickest for this. To explain what the resting length of a muscle is, stick your hands in front of you, with your palms facing you and fingers straight. Slide the fingers of each hand in between the fingers of the other hand until they touch the creases. The fingers represent the muscle fibers on a microscopic level. This is the "resting length" of your muscles after just waking up from sleep. They are tight and inflexible. Remember the stiffness you experience when you first get out of bed? Pull the fingers apart slightly. You just increased the resting length. This is what happens when you warm up. You become more flexible. The resting length of your muscles is an exact result of the activity you participate in each day. If you do nothing, the body senses that you do not want to do anything, and sets the muscle length at its minimum. When you are more active, the specific activity you do tells the muscles to "reset" the length according to the needs placed upon them. Dynamic stretching resets the resting length of your muscles each time you warm up, and over a period of four to six weeks there will be a more permanent reset of muscle length. Eventually, this will translate into *not having to warm up before participating in your training*. It takes a very long time to achieve this however.

The second phase of flexibility is actually lengthening the muscle. This takes place over several months or years of passive stretching. All passive stretching techniques come from Hatha Yoga. They just keep getting "reinvented." If you really want to develop your range of motion, strength and flexibility to promote your training in martial art, you need to practice yoga parallel to your training. Passive stretching, or yoga, provides so many benefits for your body. First, it creates a "circulatory system" for your joints. The joints have very little blood flow through them. The lymph system is the circulation. Mechanical stretching of the joints enhances the lymph flow through the joints, providing increased nutrition, metabolism and waste removal. Second, stretching increases the strength of the muscle *over its entire range of motion*. Weight training only strengthens the muscle over a small range of motion. Third, the muscles are incased in a fibrous connective tissue. This tissue must be stretched in order for the muscle to lengthen. Fourth, passive stretching also causes the tendons and ligaments to elongate and strengthen over a long period of time. The fifth benefit of passive stretching, is the conscious ability to overcome the "stretch reflex." The stretch reflex is the nervous system's way of protecting your muscles from tearing if they are stretched beyond their ability. The muscles tighten before damage occurs. The stretch reflex can be modified to sink deeper into a stretch, or to react in unison with the eccentric muscle contraction, as demonstrated in plyometrics. The sixth benefit of passive stretching is that it creates space in the joints, lowering the constant stress of compression by gravity.

The third phase of flexibility only happens after many years. Because of your constant stretching over a long period of time, your joints become very smooth and rounded where the bones and sockets meet. Your ligaments lengthen and this allows you to achieve maximum range of motion for the joint. Once you have crystalized the body in this phase, you will never lose it.

My Passive Stretching

Well into my journey in taekwondo, it seemed as though I had hit a plateau. I was very successful, and I was more flexible than many in my ring, but I could tell I was not improving any more. I went to an instructor training camp held by Chief Master Mark Sustaire in Allen, Texas. As part of the camp, he had his yoga teacher give us a one-hour class. Master Sustaire was known, and still is, to be so flexible that he could kick *straight up and break boards*. After that class, I looked down at the floor and saw I was standing in a pool of my own sweat. I could hardly do any of the poses very well, and struggled through class.

That class showed me I had a long way to go with my flexibility. Chief Master Sustaire was one of the few instructors that put an emphasis on stretching, and it showed. I went home and began to experiment with some passive stretching. After several weeks of reading books and watching videos, I came up with a simple regime that targeted the type of flexibility I needed to improve my kicking techniques. Basically, it worked on the adductor muscles of the inner thigh and the hamstrings. It also stressed the joints of the knee, ankle, and hips. The calves, back and shoulders were also stretched.

My Passive Stretching Routine

1. Twisting back flexion.

Lie on the floor on your back. Extend your arms straight out to the sides on the floor with your palms down. Lift your knees to vertical position, then lay out both knees to one side, allowing the hips to twist until the knees touch the floor. Rotate your neck as far as you can in the opposite direction. Your shoulders will tend to rise off the floor, but resist this and relax your hips and abdomen to stretch your oblique muscles and your intercostal muscles. Inhale when you lay your knees down, and exhale when you bring them up. Alternate sides. Do five repetitions. Try to relax your hip muscles.

2. Leg spreads.

Place a pillow or angled cushion under the small of your back, so your hips are somewhat elevated. With your legs pointed vertically straight, lock the knees out and pull your toes toward you. Slowly lower and relax your legs, spreading them out simultaneously to maximum split. Then bring them up together to the beginning position and repeat. After several repetitions, try to allow your legs to drop into maximum split by relaxing your adductor muscles. Allow the stretch reflex to stop the spread. Begin with about twenty repetitions, and work yourself up to one hundred. You should sense this stretch in your inner thigh and pelvis. Inhale on each spread, and exhale on each contraction.

3. Upward and downward dogs.

Kneel on the floor with hands about shoulder width apart on the floor. Raise your buttocks up in the air with your legs straight and your weight supported by your shoulders and arms. Relax your Achilles tendons, as if you were trying to touch the floor with your heels. Bring your head down looking toward your feet, as if you were trying to touch your head to your toes. Allow your shoulders to lower to the floor as far as possible. Exhale. Then lower your buttocks and raise your chest and shoulders to upward-facing dog. Lay your head all the way back on your shoulders as far as it will go. Inhale as you are doing this.

Increasing Difficulty

To make this exercise more difficult, start from an upward dog and reverse this position to downward-facing dog. Then "walk" your hands backward, keeping knees locked until you sense the stretch in your hamstrings and pressure on the balls of your feet. Hold for a moment. Keep walking backward until you reach your max stretch. Hold for a moment. If you cannot keep your palms on the floor with your knees locked out, keep your knees slightly bent and relax your lower back, with your eyes facing the floor. Hold for a few moments until your back relaxes. Now, lock your knees and try to put your hands on the floor. With your knees locked out, slowly lift your torso to vertical position. Once you get comfortable in downward-facing dog, lift one foot off the floor, and rest it on opposite calf for a few moments. Repeat with your other foot. This intensifies the Achilles tendon stretch. Do another upward and downward dog at the end of your stretch routine. As you get stronger, try to do "Snake Pushups." Begin in downward dog and lower your chest toward the floor behind your hands. Slide your chest forward in front of your hands, then raise your upper torso. Then lower your chest in front of your hands, raise your buttocks, slide your chest behind your hands, and come back to downward dog. These pushups can be hard on your shoulders if you are not used to them, but they can also really strengthen your shoulders through maximum rotation. These are great preparation for Jong Bong, sword or combat weapon training.

4. Pigeon stretches.

Use yoga blocks to support yourself at first. Assume the dog position. Bring one leg in front, knee folded underneath, with your hip lowered toward the floor. The back leg is straight behind, with the top of the foot on the floor and the heel up. Extend your hands to the side and raise your torso perpendicular to the floor. Support your torso by placing the yoga blocks under your hands if needed. Lower your front hip toward the floor until you sense the stretch in your hip joint. *You should not have any pain in your knees. The stretch should be on the outside hip joint.* Hold this position for five breaths, inhaling through the nose and exhaling through the mouth. Lower your hip joint as far as possible. Now, lower your torso and lie across your front leg, extending your arms horizontally, like in a diving posture. Hold for five breaths. Raise back up into the starting position and try to get lower into the stretch. Hold for five breaths. Repeat on other leg. As you get stronger, try to hold your torso in a vertical position without using your hands. Hold for five breaths. This stretch will really strengthen your hips and stretch your hip socket. It will improve your side kick chambers and increase power and snap in your side kicks.

5. Sitting on the heels progression.

When I became a Fifth-Degree Black Belt in taekwondo, the weapon associated with that degree was the katana or sword. The form for this weapon begins on the floor, sitting on your heels. At sixty-three years old, with both knees having been totally reconstructed, I had never been able to do this. So I began to stretch the ligaments around the knees to this position. It took me about six months to become comfortable and relaxed in this position. You, too, can do it. Simply begin by sitting on your heels, with the tops of the feet on the floor. Use blocks to support yourself upright, and hold your maximum bend for five breaths. Be sure the knees are touching each other and the buttocks are directly over your heels. Then, lift your torso forward and assume a Cobra stretch. This removes pressure from the knees and allows circulation again in the legs. Then, spread your feet slightly, while keeping your knees touching, and lean backward. This will allow your buttocks to go between your heels, slightly changing the stretch. Now lean backward as far as you can toward the floor, supporting yourself with blocks. You should sense the stretch in your quadriceps, where they insert into your knee. Try to hold this position for five breaths. Lean forward again into the Cobra stretch. Now, spread the knees to shoulder width and elevate your feet on the balls of your feet. Lean backward and try to touch your heels. Hold this position for five breaths. I won't lie, this will be difficult for most people our age at first, but gradually you will sink further into the stretch. You will get a better stretch if you warm the knees first by butt kicks or hamstring curls off the side of the bed. Once you can sit on your heels for a minute or two, you will sense the peace and tranquility this posture creates and you will begin to seek it out. This stretch and posture is great to reverse the years of compression that gravity has placed on your knees, and will increase the space within your knee joint.

6. Hamstring stretch progression.

Assume a one legged squat by kneeling on the ground and extending one leg forward as far as possible with the extended knee bent. The back leg is thrust backward with your knee and top of foot on the floor. With hands on your hips, squat down as far as possible. Sense the stretch in your groin and the bottom of the hip joint at the insertion of the hamstring. Sense the stretch in your rear leg where the quadriceps are inserted into the hip. Hold for five breaths. Then lean your torso forward with your shoulder inside the forward knee. Support yourself with your hand or elbow on the floor. Hold for five breaths. Now shift your torso back and sit on your back heel. Straighten out your front leg with your toes arched backward toward your face. Grab your toes, or try to, and lean forward as far as you can. Sense the stretch in your hamstring. Hold this posture for a moment. Now come up, keeping the back straight, and extend the front leg out as far forward as you can into a hamstring stretch. Use blocks to support your weight if you have to and be sure your torso is vertical. Slide into your max stretch and hold this for five breaths. Now, bend forward and lean your torso over the extended leg. This will intensify the stretch. Hold for five breaths. Supporting yourself by hands or blocks, release yourself from the stretch and repeat on the other leg. As you get more flexible, there are many variations you can use to broaden the stretch to the outer and inner thigh to increase the length of *all of the muscles, tendons and ligaments around the hip.* One such variation, while in max front split stretch, is to roll your hip to the outside and allow it to lay on the floor. Support your torso with a hand or block and lean forward over the leg to grab your toes with your opposite hand. Hold for five breaths. Resume front split, then lean torso to inside of the extended leg. Put your hands on the floor to support your weight, then lean forward and push your front heel outward. Sense the stretch on the inside of the thigh, in the adductor muscles. Hold for five breaths. Now, try to put your pubis on the floor by stretching the torso farther out away from the forward leg. Sense the stretch in your sartorius and adductor muscles. Hold for five breaths. This is your main stretch for hamstrings and adductors. Do this stretch last. If you have noticed, all prior stretches are to prepare you for this stretch.

7. Side split progression.

Stand with your feet together and bend forward to try to touch your toes. Hold for three breaths. Come up and spread the front of your feet to the side, then bring your heels in line with your toes. Go down again and try to touch the floor. Hold for three breaths. Repeat this toe/heel outward spread until you can put your head on the floor. At this point, you may have to support your torso with your hands. During this outward spread of the legs, hold one breath in center, then lean over to each leg and touch your toes or hold your torso against that leg. Hold each side for one breath. When you get your side split as far as possible, support your stretch with your hands or yoga blocks. Extend your stretch to the max while supported on yoga blocks. Hold for three breaths. Then, lift your toes off the ground and rest your weight on your heels only. Sink deeper into the stretch. Hold for three breaths. Continue until max stretch. Hold for three breaths. Then, lower your buttocks to the floor. Now lean forward and place your hands on the floor as far forward as you can. You should sense the stretch in your adductor muscles. Hold until uncomfortable, then try to touch your toes on each leg, one leg at a time. Then inch each leg outward on the heel to increase the stretch. Go down again in the middle and on each leg. Do three repetitions of this stretch until you have reached your max. Now, with hands behind your hips, pull yourself out of the stretch and relax.

Connecting It All Together

As with any endeavor, physical, emotional, intellectual or spiritual (the spiritual being a harmonic combination of the first three), you *must practice daily for forty days to increase your level of being.* You must persevere through time to gain *force.* To say it another way, *you are what you do every day.* You are not what you think, what you feel, what you imagine nor what you hope for. Hanging in my dojang is a reminder from the man who changed everything about my life. It reads as follows.

> *"Man is a being that does.*
> *That is a man.*
> *It is not one who thinks or feels or cries 'Lord, Lord.'*
> *He is one who does.*
> *It is he who makes what he knows into a reality of doing.*
> *Then a man can experience his being."*
> —W. A. NYLAND

Make stretching part of your life. Watch your martial art grow accordingly. Remember the Rites? They started off slow and increased gradually. This is how you should approach stretching. With dynamic stretching, if you can't do ten repetitions to begin, start with what you can do and then gradually increase until you find the level that propels you into class with confidence! Experiment and find the stretches that expose your weaknesses. Do those stretches first and try to double your repetitions. Eventually your weaknesses will be your strength! Remember that you will gain *force* by struggling with your weaknesses! You will develop *will* from the *struggle between yes and no.*

With passive stretching, there are many ways to approach the postures. The first way is to increase your time in each posture when you reach your *max stretch*. This is where muscle fascia gets the signal that you want it to elongate. If the max stretch is difficult, hold it for one breath only. Then work your way up to five breaths. Some people really put emphasis on the time in a stretch, sometimes up to thirty seconds. If it works for you, do it. However, the pain can be excruciating and the soreness afterward prolonged. For me, I have found that it is just as important to learn how to relax the muscle into the max stretch.

Another way to increase your stretch is by isometric stretching. This is done by reaching your max stretch for any muscle or group of muscles, and then tensing that muscle for five to ten seconds (or equivalent breaths). Then relax the muscle and you should sink deeper into the stretch. This method actually *deactivates the stretch reflex for a few seconds after the tensing,* allowing you to sink deeper into the stretch. Be careful, this method can cause damage and great soreness to the muscles if overdone. This technique can be executed up to three repetitions for each stretch.

A third way to increase your stretch is to alternate is to the stretch with relaxation. Get in your max stretch, then relax the stretch for a moment, then go back to the max stretch. You should sink slightly more into your max stretch. This can also be done for up to three repetitions for each stretch.

Finally, use your breath. This is one of the most misunderstood or least understood and least practiced techniques in martial art. *Life is breath.* The way it was explained to me was that air is our second food. Solid and liquid food is the first. A person can live for forty days without food, but we can't live for four minutes without air. Just as our body extracts nutrients for its growth and maintenance, so we extract nutrients from the air, not just oxygen. I will not go into this further. If you are interested, there are some references in the appendix. Several martial arts use breathing techniques, like ki-hap. Abdominal breathing is something you must strive to practice. It is different from mechanical intercostal breathing. Intercostal breathing, or breathing by the expansion of your rib cage, only allows about one-tenth (0.1) liter of air to enter your lungs. *Abdominal breathing allows one full liter of air to enter your lungs!* Practice abdominal breathing in the Rites, in your stretching and in your training. With the Rites and stretching, inhale through the nose and exhale through the mouth. This simple method extracts more nutrients. Inhale before exertion, and exhale during the exertion. You will notice that you slip deeper into your stretch each time. You will also reduce the pain of your stretch. You will gain *force*. Remember, breath can enhance technique or retard technique. The actual use of breath is always a conscious effort.

I remember we had a student that trained with us that had asthma. He used an inhaler before class. I sparred with him several times and was impressed with his performance as he coped with his condition. Once after class, I asked him how he could maintain such exertion with his condition. His explanation has been a roadmap for me of this most essential and most blessed activity of simply breathing.

"Sometimes it is just a matter of you becoming tired of breathing because of exertion. I trained in how to maximize my ability to allow air to enter and exit my lungs. I begin by consciously depressing my diaphragm under my lungs to create a vacuum that pulls air into my lungs. After my lungs became full with this technique, I expand my ribcage. This combination increased the flow of air to the greatest possible volume possible for me. In this way, I have been able to participate in sparring, which I value considerably, almost to the level of other people."

Dynamic Stretching Routine

Upper Body

Neck rotations through entire range of motion. Ten repetitions each.

Front and back   **Side to side**

Over and back

360 degree rotations left and right. Do slowly, only five repetitions.

The neck is one of the first parts of the physical body to lose its range of motion. A flexible neck is important in change of direction and reverse techniques in martial art. You must look first before you do. Stiffness in the neck is a sign of a very restricted range of motion and contracting of your envelope of being. It has been said that an inflexibility in the body is a reflection of inflexibility in the mind.

Shoulder rotations through entire range of motion

Running in place

Pec decks

Windmills

Sky waves

Trunk rotations

Dynamic Stretching

Lower Body

Buttocks kicks   **Straight leg swings**

Straight leg raises

Knee strikes   **Side kick chambers**

Ten repetitions each side, keep guard up

Outer crescent kick

Side kick leg swings

Side kicks

Leg Spreads

Begin on the floor with something under your sacrum, like a pillow, yoga block or your own hands. Spread your legs and allow them to fall outward. Start slowly until your hamstrings and adductors start to relax, then let your legs free fall until the stretch reflex stops the spread. Begin with twenty repetitions and work yourself up to one hundred. After a period of time, add one pound to each ankle and work yourself up to one hundred again. Be sure to keep your knees locked out. Continue to add weight in one pound intervals until you achieve the stretch you are looking for. Do not overdo it. You are looking to relax your hamstrings and adductors into all kicks.

Hamstring Curls

Begin on the side of your bed in the morning or use a bench. Extend your leg so that your knee is just free of the bed or bench.. There are two positions, one with your heel extended and one with the balls of your feet extended, like in a front kick. Start with twenty repetitions with heel extended and then twenty with ball of the foot extended. Work your way up to one hundred, fifty in each position and on each foot. After that, put a one pound weight on your ankles. Work your way up to one hundred. Keep adding weight until you can do one hundred repetitions on each foot with a five pound ankle weight. You are ready for anything now.

These last two dynamic stretches are usually done at home, right after waking up.

Passive Stretching

Frog Stretches

Frog stretches isolate the adductor muscles of the groin and ligaments of the hip joints. There are two basic postures, one with feet almost touching and the other with feet parallel to each other. To settle into your max stretch, move your torso slightly forward which will deepen the stretch and then push your buttocks back to really stress the hip joint. The leg parallel position works the hip joint from slightly different angle. You should do these stretches often for they loosen the ligaments around the hip joints and open up your hips. This stretch will improve your side kick chambers.

Pidgeon Stretches

Bend your front knee underneath the front leg with the heel up in front of the groin. The rear leg is extended directly behind your buttocks. Relax your hip slightly to the outside of the front leg and sense the stress on the hip joint. There should be NO KNEE PAIN. Then lean over the front leg toward the inside and go to the floor. Again, roll you hip to the outside to stress the hip joint again. Repeat this stretch on the other hip. If your back is stiff, you may have difficulty with holding your torso vertically. This stretch is great for side kick chambers and for extensions that require hip rotation for proper technique.

Hamstring Progressions

Begin with both knees on the floor, then extend the front leg forward, knee bent, into a lunge. Sink down in the hips in order to stress the insertion of the front hamstring and insertion of the quadriceps in the rear leg. Then bend the torso down inside the knee to stress the adductors and the Sartorius muscle. After relaxing into the max stretch for these two postures, come back and sit on the knee while extending the front leg straight out to stretch the front hamstring. Then bend over front leg and grab the toes to deepen the stretch.

Next, raise up and extend the front leg straight out in front of you as far as it will go with the heel on the ground. Relax into the stretch by pushing the heel further out while maintaining your balance. Now bend over the front leg to stress the hamstrings even more. Settle to the floor onto the hip and lean over and grab the toes. This stresses the outside hamstring. Then, while keeping the leg extended, roll the hips to the inside and try to put your pubis on the floor. This stretches your inner hamstring and your adductor muscles. If you have any trouble with these postures, use yoga blocks to support yourself until you are flexible enough without them. Repeat on the other leg. This progression isolates and works every angle of the hamstrings.

Hamstrings are THE most important muscles to develop for kicking techniques.

Side Split Progression

Begin upright and bend down and try to touch your toes with feet together. Then open the front of your feet and then kick your heels out (walking out). Try to touch the floor. Hold each stretch until your muscles relax.

Continue walking out, bending to the floor with each increment. Relax into each stretch. When you get wide enough, you can hold on to your ankles for stability and slide further out. When you can, put your forehead on the floor. At this point, all the pressure is on your adductor muscles and sartorius.

When you reach your max stretch, support yourself with your arms and relax. Then rotate your hips to lift up on your heels and again slide out to your max stretch. The pressure is all on your hamstrings now. Be patient with this progression and relax into your max stretch with each posture.

Now support yourself with your hands and continue to widen the stretch until you reach your max stretch. If you can do a full split you can stop here. If not, lower yourself slowly until you reach the floor in your max side split stretch.

Once on the ground, lean forward to put more stress on your adductors. Relax into the stretch. Then lean over each leg as far as you can and grab your toes and relax into the stretch. When finished, use your arms to inch one leg out as far as you can and repeat the lean forward and the lean to each side. Repeat the inch out for three cycles. This is the end of the side split progression. To exit this position, do not force your legs inward. Instead, use your arms to push your buttocks backward to release the pressure on your legs.

This side split progression will target all the areas needed to eventually do a side split and it will strengthen and elongate all angles of your adductors and hamstrings.

Sitting on Heels

Kneel on floor with your torso erect. Gently settle down with your buttocks sitting on your heels. If you cannot go all the way down, use yoga blocks to support yourself or place a pad or pillow under your buttocks. Then try to relax into the posture. It took me about six months to be able to achieve this posture with relaxation. However, once you can do this you will enjoy a sense of peace and total relaxation of body, mind and feeling. When you are ready, lean forward into a cobra posture to allow circulation back into your knees.

Next, spread your legs slightly and come back up over your knees. But this time sink your buttocks in between your heels and lean your torso as far back as you can while supporting yourself with your arms. Tilt your head as far back as it can go. You should sense a definite stretch in your quadriceps muscles where they insert into your knees. When you are ready, go back into the cobra to release the tension. Finally, spread your legs a little wider, and come back up, but this time with your toes on the floor. Arch your back as far as it will go while supporting your torso with your hands on your heels. Slide down the back of your feet as far as you can go, with head all the way back. This is a very good torso stretch.

The importance of these stretches cannot be ignored. It is vital that you begin to increase the space between the knees. This space decreases as you age and your knees will continue to deteriorate without your efforts. Your knees need to get stronger as you go through martial art to prevent injury as kicking techniques become more and more difficult. This is especially true with spinning and jumping kicks. These stretches will improve circulation within the joint and strengthen your knee ligaments and the tendons that attach the leg muscles to your knees. I do these stretches after a workout as part of my passive stretching routine. I do them between the hamstring progression and side split progression when my knees are very warm. I only started doing them at fifth degree black belt. My sword form required this posture to begin the form. I regret that I did not begin them earlier in my career. If I had, I feel they might have prevented the knee injuries I sustained in earlier belts.

Torso Stretches

Begin on floor with knees up. Allow knees to fall to one side while head goes the other direction. Hold until fully relaxed, then repeat on the other side. Keep knees together. This stretches your oblique, latissimus dorsa and intercostal muscles. This stretch and trunk rotations, shown in dynamic stretching, are the basis for all reverses.

Shoulder Stretches

This is a yoga posture called "Threading the Needle." In addition to stretching the shoulders it also twists the upper body to loosen the oblique muscles. Begin in dog posture, then thread the shoulder underneath the support arm. Lift free arm to increase stretch. You may have to adjust torso to place stress on shoulder instead of neck. Repeat on other side. This stretch is preparing your torso and shoulders for the punching, blocking and weapon techniques that put tremendous stresses on your shoulders.

Upward and Downward Dogs

These stretches work almost all the muscles of the body. Begin in dog posture. Then raise your buttocks straight up as high as you can go. Press your head and neck down between your shoulders and look between your legs. You should sense the stretch in your shoulders, back, buttocks, hamstrings, calves and feet. Try to keep your heels on the floor. Exhale with this posture and hold for a moment. Then let your hips and torso drop to the floor but not touch it. Arch your back and lift your head back to look at the ceiling. This should be a relaxed posture with a good stretch in your abdomen, rib cage and pelvis. Inhale with this posture and hold for a moment. Repeat as many times as you wish.

Chapter 4

*Always strive to combine
the necessary and the useful.*

INJURY PREVENTION
AND RECOVERY

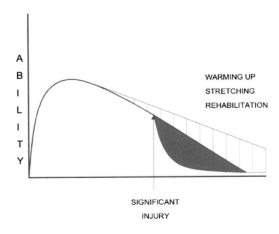

SIGNIFICANT

INJURY

RECOVERY TIME

Injuries

Competitive taekwondo is an extreme practice. It assaults your physical, emotional and mental envelopes. Conceptually, your envelope can be thought of as a two or three dimensional geometric shape with the ten attributes at the edges. The ten attributes I absorbed from the practice of taekwondo, expounded by the American Taekwondo Association are: Attitude, proper technique, balance, eye contact, focus, speed, power, rhythm and movement, timing, and automatic movement. As each attribute grows, the shape of the figure changes. The area within the boundary can be called the totality of your being, or your individuality. Therein lies one of the great benefits of martial art. You grow as an individual - physically, emotionally, mentally and possibly spiritually in the sense of being. Physically speaking, you develop strength, balance, flexibility, speed and power in all of the parts of the body. This type of growth is not easy, and it takes time and perseverance. It is not without injury, either. Injury does not take place because of an inherent danger of the practice, but because the practitioner does not understand the nature of the effort needed to grow without overdoing it. Gradually, you learn to refine your practice and to go up to the edge of your envelope and not to break through it, thereby injuring yourself. Also, this growth does not take place linearly or smoothly. It is characterized by pulses of training (which are defined by the quality and quantity of effort) which appear as growth, setbacks and plateaus (which appear as defeat, disillusion or lack of wish). This learning curve constantly changes as you graduate through a succession of belts. The postures, strikes, kicks and blocks become ever more difficult, and require increased strength, power and flexibility, especially when you get to jumping and spinning kicks.

As a senior practitioner, you enter the martial art world with your envelope fixed by habits of the previous 40-50 years of life. As opposed to being young, you are no longer growing and developing, but you are deteriorating. You are stiff and rigid, and fixed by repetitions of your daily life. Basically, the practice of martial art must maintain or improve your capacities beyond ordinary life, and you must struggle to grow in the face of the Eternal Heropass (time).

I began taekwondo when I was forty-four. I could not raise my leg and put it on the kitchen counter. I could not sit on my knees, or touch the floor with my hands or balance on one foot. All of my joints were tight, my back stiff, and my shoulders could not rotate back all the way. Whenever I kicked or threw a punch, I lost my balance. I assume that you, my dear reader, are in similar shape. I did not know how to warm up, stretch or cool down. I was overweight and did not know how to exert myself without injury. My instructor was twenty years younger than me and had no idea of what someone my age needed. And how could he have? The curriculum was geared to children and young adults.

As a result, I incurred many injuries, suffered a lot of pain and lost a lot of training time in recovery. Since I worked full time as a pharmacist, I suffered a lot by having to work with the pain of my injuries while having to stand all day and fill prescriptions. I broke toes, I broke my wrist, I got my finger kicked off (no lie), I got plantar fasciitis three times, I blew out both of my ACLs (anterior cruciate ligament), I tore my hamstring in half and tore the rotator cuff on my shoulder.

The aim of this chapter is to go through each injury and tell you how I rehabilitated from it to continue the martial art journey. In addition, I am going to show you how I feel I could have prevented these injuries. It is my wish that you can learn from my mistakes and have a long and injury free experience in martial art.

Broken Toes

When you start to break boards, it is possible you will be required to break them with front kicks. Proper technique for board breaking with front kicks is to retract your toes upward and backward, thereby striking the board with the ball of your foot instead of your toes. The problem with seniors, is that by this time in their lives usually their toes cannot bend backward very much. It is possible that they have already been injured or have other problems. When I was a brown belt, I was required to break two boards with a jump front kick at face level. Looking back, it seems that I was always trying to do more than needed, like trying to break every board on my right and left side. Well, my left toe would not retract all the way, so I broke it. In addition to the regular recovery time, the swelling in the big metatarsal joint did not go down for years and later on it caused other foot problems which I still deal with today. There is not much you can do with broken toes except to let them heal. The real secret is preventative stretching. The best exercise is the upward and downward dogs, the most common yoga position. If you do these stretches beginning with your first class, for three times a week, after a year you will be able to fully retract your toes for a safe front kick. If you want to prevent injury, have good front kick technique and not have foot trouble for the rest of your life, you must put in the time to make your toes flexible. We will talk about this stretch again and again, for it has many beneficial results in preventing multiple injuries from the more advanced techniques you will encounter in your martial art journey. A more advanced stretch is sitting on the floor on your knees and the balls of the feet. The most advanced is a back bend with your knees and balls of the feet on the floor. Even after injury, you can regain most or all of your full joint rotation by dedicated stretching over a long period of time.

Dropped Metatarsals

Doctors say this condition is common in seniors, but it took me by surprise how quickly it came about and how severe this can be. It is when one or more of the metatarsal heads "drop" or get lower than the others. Metatarsals are the long bones in your feet. The metatarsal heads connect these long bones with the bones of the toe, forming the "ball" of the foot. When it manifests itself, it is like walking everywhere with a marble always under the ball of your foot. The pain prevents you from walking at all on hardwood floors or concrete. Twisting and turning the ball of your foot when doing kicks is excruciating. The less foot pad you have, the more sensitive it is to normal walking and standing activities. I do not know how to prevent this and neither do the doctors. I tried pads of all sorts, shoes of all kinds, and almost every insole available. The only thing that has worked for me and has allowed me to train and compete is a Dr. Scholl's foot pad. I cut two pads to the shape of my metatarsal crescent and taped them to hold them in place. I invented this taping method myself and the foot doctor was enthusiastic about the result. This method of taping allowed me to train normally and compete for the rest of my career.

Plantar Fasciitis

My first introduction to this scourge was when we had a young "hot shot" sixteen-year-old guest warm up our class. His "warm up" consisted of a fifteen minute period of jumping techniques on our floor that had a single layer of outdoor carpet over concrete. Four adult students, including my wife and myself, came down with plantar fasciitis. My feet still ache when I remember this episode. This "devilish delicacy" is a lengthy trauma for any athlete. I had it three times. The plantar fascia is a tough connective tissue under each foot. It connects each metatarsal with the calcaneus or heel bone. It absorbs all of the weight of the body with each step. If it is subjected to a strain beyond its strength, it tears. These tears can be small or complete. Usually the tears are small and become inflamed, and sometimes swelling takes place under the foot. The usual tear is right at the point of the heel, so that each step is painful on the heel. At first, you may not acknowledge the pain except for the first few steps when you first get out of bed each morning. This is because your muscles, tendons and fascia cool and contract at night causing stiffness in the morning. As you move around and warm up, there tends to be less pain, or maybe just a constant aching. Doctors usually prescribe anti-inflammatory drugs that help the pain somewhat but do nothing for the condition. After these don't work, then they give you a steroid shot in the heel, which may help the pain for a few weeks but does not cure the condition. The truth is that it takes almost exactly one year of suffering for it to heal. The best treatment is to reduce the stress on your heel and make it as comfortable as possible. Do these things.

1. Get and wear the most supportive pair of tennis shoes you can buy. Be sure to buy your shoes in the afternoon and not in the morning. Your feet will swell during the day and if they fit in the morning, they will be too tight in the afternoon.

2. Get the best pair of insoles you can buy and add them to your shoe padding. The best ones I have found are sold by Riecken's Orthotic Laboratory. They are a special viscous, elastic gel butterfly tri-laminate insole. Be sure to take your insoles with you when you buy your shoes so that you will have enough room for a comfortable fit.

3. Elevate your foot above your heart every night and ice it for at least thirty minutes to reduce the swelling that has accumulated during the day. Because gravity holds the swelling in your feet, you must reduce it every night by using gravity to drain it and therefore reduce the swelling.

4. Stretch your plantar fascia three times a day, every day. For me, the most valuable stretches are the wall stretches and the upward and downward dogs.

5. Tape your foot every day if you have a job that requires standing, and tape it before each workout. Taping spreads out the force of your weight over the whole area of your foot. Only train on padded floors or mats.

Prevention of Plantar Fasciitis

The origin of plantar fasciitis is a "tight" plantar fascia, caused by the lack of athletic activity in your life. In martial art, you will absorb tremendous stresses on your feet from twisting and jumping. A single episode of jumping can lead to this injury. Prevention of this dreaded condition should begin when you start your martial art training. The major emphasis is on stretching and elongating the plantar fascia. This will prevent this condition. The single best stretch is downward and upward dogs. Wall stretches are also good. Do your stretches at least three times per week and before each training. Modify your warm up to suit your own level of fitness.

Hamstring Pulls and Tears

The importance of your hamstring muscles in martial art cannot be underestimated, especially in seniors. All kicking techniques are an orchestration between all the muscles of your upper and lower leg, hip, abdomen and back. The hamstring muscles are the centerpiece of your kicks. In order to extend your lower leg and lock out your knees, the hamstring muscles must stretch out fully. In order to prevent ligament injury, they it must prevent hyperextension that results from the snapping action of kicks. In order to do that, they must lock your knee securely when you stand on your plant foot while kicking, otherwise the strain will be transmitted to your ligaments. The hamstrings maintain your balance with one foot off the floor. The height of all of your kicks is limited by the length and resilience of the hamstrings and adductor muscles. With such importance placed on a muscle group by a martial art that is known for powerful kicking techniques, does it not seem that a special emphasis would be placed upon their development? Sadly, I never heard a word about the significance that flexible hamstrings have in your training. I had to learn the hard way.

The year was 1994 at the World Championships. I was a first degree black belt competing in sparring. We were competing on a carpeted floor. I was ahead when I came down awkwardly from a kick and slipped on the carpet. The result was a full front split. "Pop," I tore my hamstring in half. I finished the fight, but lost, because I could only stand on one foot and punch defensively. Even with pain pills and ice, the eight-hour ride home was agonizing and depressing. The doctor said I could have my hamstring surgically repaired, but I declined because I had to go back to work and could not take the time off for the surgery. Being a pharmacist, I had to stand for ten hours every day. I had to drag my leg around, swollen like a poisoned pup, with a huge hematoma from my hamstring tear that settled in my foot. I suffered for about two months before it began to heal, and it was nine months before I could compete again. One good thing was that my flexibility increased with that hamstring, because the tear healed together in two different places. The second good thing was that I realized that I needed to prepare my leg muscles a great deal more before I entered the ring.

Knee Injuries

Of all of the injuries I have sustained over the years, the knee injury called Anterior Cruciate Ligament (ACL) tear was the most devastating. It required surgery and a lengthy and painful rehabilitation, accompanied by emotional and mental stress. You cannot compete for six to nine months, and it is very possible you will lose your nerve and never compete again. Once again, the main cause is the lack of strength and flexibility of your hamstrings and the adductor muscles in relation to your quadriceps. Your quadriceps are about eight times stronger than your hamstrings. This translates into tremendous stress on the knee ligaments when you lock out your knee on the plant leg with your kicks. The stress on the ligaments is even more when you do spin kicks or jumping kicks and land on one leg. The reason for this contrast between the strength of the quadriceps and hamstrings is the sedimentary nature of most people. The quadriceps are used in standing up from a sitting position and sitting back down. But the hamstrings are rarely used unless you run, bike or swim. Even this type of exercise does not prepare your hamstrings for taekwondo kicking. The hamstrings must be consciously trained over a long period of time in order to protect your knees. If you started martial arts in your forties or fifties, then it is very likely that you have weak hamstrings.

If you look at the anatomy of the hamstrings, the distal (knee) insertions of the tendons come around each side of the knee joint and stabilize that joint when standing on one foot. If the strength of your hamstrings does not approach the strength of your quadriceps, then tremendous stresses are placed upon the ACL, PCL (Posterior Cruciate Ligament) and the Meniscus cartilage to lock out your knee. If the forces are too great, you will get a strain or tear in one of the participants. Believe me, most knee problems occur from weak hamstrings.

In 1999, I was in the Top Ten for the first time in my martial art career. I had just turned second degree black belt and was practicing the Jong Bong form (midrange staff). At the end of the form, you have to squat down on your back leg and slam the Jong Bong on the floor, while extending the front leg. My knee was not ready for this movement and I heard the dreaded "pop." It didn't hurt that much at first, and I continued to train for the world championships, but the pain and swelling began to recur, especially after training sessions. I took anti-inflammatory drugs and iced it every night after training, but it only got worse. Eventually, I had to stop training and became depressed. I had intentionally trained for the World Championships for six months, and now this injury could keep me from the competition. Back then, the coveted crown was the All-Around World Champion. To be in the Top Ten you had to accumulate points in forms and sparring, obtained from five regional tournaments and two national tournaments. The final competition (World Championships) was in Little Rock, Arkansas where the Top Ten competitors were required to spar-off for the crown. After a lot of rest and experimentation, about the only thing I could do while sparring was a right side kick with my left leg as plant leg. As it turned out, all those thousands of sidekicks I had practiced came in handy, and I won all four rounds with the sidekicks and punches only. This would be much food for thought for me later on. I celebrated, but still had pain, inflammation and swelling in my right knee. The next tournament was in Lufkin, Texas on a wooden gymnasium floor. Rodney Tooley and I were locked in a tie while sparring for first place. I came down from a kick on my right knee and went straight to the floor. I could not go on. When I got home, I went to see Dr. Bramhall, the orthopedic surgeon for the Texas A&M football team. He examined my knee and said, "Torn ACL, do you want me to fix it?"

I said yes, and he gave me a complete ACL reconstruction, giving me a choice between my patellar or hamstring tendon. The patellar was the stronger of the two, so I chose patellar. After a week, I was back at work again, standing for ten hours with a knee brace. I still remember that time, keeping my knee straight, swollen like a log, walking around like Chester in the TV program *Gunsmoke*. After three months of this, along with rehabilitation exercises three times a week, I gradually removed the brace. Rehabilitation exercises were aimed at regaining 180 degree flexion and strengthening the muscles of the upper and lower leg. After that I was on my own. After much reading and consultation with the surgeon who had done the operation, I concentrated on the development of my hamstrings. Each morning before getting out of bed, I would lay on my belly and extend my leg over the edge of the bed, just past the knee joint. Then I did hamstring curls, concentrating on full extension and full contraction. I worked my way up to 100 repetitions on each leg, fifty with my toes drawn back like a heel kick and fifty with my foot extended but the toes drawn back like a front kick. After I reached 100 repetitions, I added a one pound of weight on my ankle and worked my way up to 100 reps again on each leg. Again and again, after achieving 100 repetitions, I increased the weight until I could do a hundred reps with five pounds. In the meantime, several times a week I would lay on the floor and do all of my kicks in slow motion for ten to twenty repetitions on each side. I would do front kicks, sidekicks, hook kicks and round kicks while concentrating on technique. At five months into recovery, there came the "psychological part," that is, you had to find out what you can do and what you cannot do. The way I approached this "Fa Bridge," was a thought process that unfolded like this. "If and when I could do my full, dynamic warm up, that I had done for many years, then I would be ready to do my form segments again." To my surprise and relief, I found that I could do my dynamic warm up, and so I added it to my rehabilitation. After six months I resumed form practice, beginning with White Belt, until I could do each segment three to five times. Gradually from there, I went through all the forms until I could complete Second Degree Black Belt form several times in a row. Then I started choreographing my sparring moves on the heavy bag. After seven months, I resumed class without anything on my knee but a neoprene sleeve. I was still in the Top Ten due to my success at the World Championships from the previous year. I went back to Worlds and I won my second World Title in sparring.

This experience taught me many things. First, I realized that I would not lose my previous training, even after a long layoff. I only needed to refine the "connections" between my body and my mind that were unused for many months. Second, I realized that I had developed that most misunderstood attribute called "will," to a tremendous level because of my previous training. It became evident when I was injured and could not use this mental-emotional force for training and competition. So I applied it to rehabilitation. I realized that this "conscious effort" is never lost - it is transformed into a higher level of "being" and a fresh supply of energy for work.

In 2006, I became a Fourth Degree Black Belt. The most difficult technique in that form with seniors is no doubt the step-jump-spin heel kick. In this respect, I cannot pass by in silence a most important physiological law pertaining to the ratio of the center of gravity and height. The difficulty with jump spinning kicks is that the forces on the body increase exponentially with a geometric increase in height. As the height and length of the limbs (arms and legs) increase, the stability of the spinning body decreases because of a higher center of gravity along the vertical axis of the body. The centrifugal force generated by the longer limbs pulls the body outward during the spin. The potential for wobbling increases, causing the practitioner to land at an unbalanced angle when finishing his kick. This inherent instability is magnified by a lack of flexibility, causing the body to lean back as the kick is executed. Landing without balance can be devastating for the foot, ankle, and especially the knee, hip and back. In one sense, martial art and jumping kicks have been developed and refined by cultures of Asian origin. Their bodies have a better harmony in their proportions, which translates into incredible jumping and spinning kicks. Taller people, like me, have much more difficulty in these techniques because of the increase in proportions and the increases in centrifugal force generated by the spin. I did not know that in 2007. I was trying to do this kick like my instructor Master Michael Pak, who is a 5' 8" Korean. This was a mistake that would cost me another blown ACL, this time on my left knee, and the loss of another nine months of training. While practicing one day, my left leg landed at an angle, tearing my ACL completely in two. I heard a definite "pop," and after that I could not walk without assistance. I knew immediately what had happened, and my heart sank into my stomach. However, since I had done it before, I knew what had to be done. Again I rehabilitated, resumed martial art, made a comeback and regained my crown as World Champion in sparring. Think about this if you are tall and reach fourth degree Black Belt.

How to Recover from Torn ACL

1. Do not despair or give up.

2. Go to the best sports surgeon there is and get it fixed.

3. Rehab exactly as the doctor and rehab specialist show you.

4. Begin strengthening and stretching your hamstring muscles to where they are *stronger than before the injury.*

5. Never stop strengthening and stretching your hamstrings, and *all* of your leg, hip, back and shoulder muscles, while you practice martial art.

6. *Always strive to combine the necessary and the useful.* You may not be able to do kicks while you are in rehab, but you can do sit-ups, punching and blocking techniques. Use this time to grow in your hand techniques. You will be better than you ever were when you resume.

7. Reaffirm your aim in martial art, to be World Champion.

How to Prevent ACL Injuries

1. Begin a stretching and strengthening program as soon as you enter martial art, especially with your hamstring muscles. Never stop.

2. Learn to do all of your color belt techniques correctly before you get to black belt. Poor technique will lead you to many injuries.

3. Be sure to have a good instructor (one who can do the techniques) to teach you the advanced jumps, kicks and spinning techniques. *I cannot stress this enough. Your instructor is the most important influence in your martial art journey until YOU take on that responsibility.*

4. Practice all your kicking techniques at least once a week.

5. Practice your martial art on mats that are at least one inch thick.

6. Whenever you sense a pain that does not go away in one day, *rest until it does*. If it does not go away, see your sports doctor specialist immediately.

Shoulder Injuries

Your shoulders are very important, for they are the "handle of the whip," so to speak. When punching, striking and blocking, the energy of the hips, torso and muscles of the chest and back funnel their energy through your shoulders. Not only do they transmit this energy, but they also have to stop it at the end of the technique. If you add a weapon or weapons to the hands, the forces on the shoulders are multiplied manifold. As with all the joints, a good warm up is needed to prevent injuries. The warm up should include all possible movements of the shoulders.

When combat weapon sparring was introduced, an entirely new stress was placed on my shoulders, which up until then had been relatively injury-free. Unfortunately, I developed a chronic shoulder problem when I did my fit test as a Fourth Degree Black Belt in 2008. The combination of pushups and punches left with me a chronic pain in my shoulder whenever I lifted my arm straight up and over my head. High X blocks hurt like crazy, pushups were painful and double outer forearm blocks and circular blocks made me wince every time when I was bringing them to a stop. Even sleeping on it was painful. I tried to rest for two months, alternate ice and heat on it and I took anti-inflammatory drugs, all with no effect. I went to my sports surgeon, and he said it was a ligament strain in my rotator cuff. So I did rehab exercises for two months and it improved somewhat, but it did not go away. I was preparing to test for my Fifth Degree Black Belt in 2010, and worried that it would not heal in time. Then I got a thirty-minute massage every week for four weeks, and the pain was significantly diminished, but it was still there. Finally, I followed up with a chiropractor for the first time in my life. She gave me acupuncture once a week for three weeks. One day, after three weeks, I realized my pain was gone! I tested and got my fifth degree in 2010.

In 2012, combat weapon sparring was introduced and I was successful enough to get into the Top Ten and went to the World Championships in 2013. I sparred the required four rounds and won the first Combat

Weapon World Title in the 60-99 year old ring. The next day my arm was extremely sore, and on Sunday I competed again for the new competition year. I sparred three rounds, but lost in the third round because my shoulder hurt so much that I could not overcome the pain to fight effectively. The pain did not go away, and so I went back to my surgeon. He said it was a partial tear in my rotator cuff, but he did not recommend surgery at my age (65) because of poor recovery outcomes and he said I would have a chronic stiffness in my shoulder that would plague me for the rest of my life. So I plunged into rehab again. I had weekly massages and acupuncture treatments and after two months it worked. Now I had the roadmap to recovery for all strains and partial tears of ligaments. I also realized that six months is a realistic time to allow for recovery. After that, I began to strengthen my shoulders by doing yoga (upward and downward dogs), light weight training (bench presses, flies and presses) and Bahng Mahng Ee drills with "live" bamboo sticks. Later I got a suburito (a wooden training sword) and did strengthening exercises with it. In 2014, I won my second consecutive World Title in combat weapons, and in 2015, I won my third World Title in a row.

In order to alert you to the stresses that are put on your shoulder during combat weapon sparring, you must realize that each fight requires around 100 swings of the weapon as hard as you can, with many of the strikes not hitting anything. It is then that the shoulder must absorb the abrupt stop and change in direction of the weapon while twisting and torqueing the rotator cuff. If it is not ready for such stresses, you are going to hurt your shoulder.

Back Injuries

As a pharmacist, I have twenty or more patients on various pain medications for back problems at any one time. It makes me so thankful that so far I do not have such problems. I know taekwondo practitioners that have back problems and their abilities and flexibility are limited. For me, I am reminded that the same stretching and strengthening exercises of yoga are something I needed to continually practice to prevent back injuries. I have had minor bouts of back strain, mostly in the lumbar region. The treatment is the same as for shoulder problems - rest, pain medication, muscle relaxants, chiropractor adjustments, yoga stretching, massage and acupuncture.

Knee Rehabilitation

Hamstring Curls

Begin by laying on a bench or bed stomach down. Extend your knee over the side so that the knee joint is very close to the bench but without being directly on it. Push your toes straight down and your heel up, and lock the foot in this way. Lift your leg to vertical or beyond, while holding your toes down, as if you were doing a hook kick. Then lower the leg down to the original position. Repeat this motion twenty times, or until you get fatigued. Now change the position of your foot by pointing the toes so that the foot is extended straight back. This works the hamstrings at a slightly different angle. If you do not have shoes on, roll your toes back, exposing the ball of the foot as if you were going to strike a board with a front kick. Now, repeat this motion twenty more times or until you get fatigued. After you get familiar with these motions, increase the speed of the cycle, as if you were doing a hook-kick, round-kick combination. Over time, work yourself up to one hundred repetitions on each leg. A good time to do these is in the morning before getting out of bed. Just slide over the side of the bed, belly down, and do them before you get up. Once you achieve a one-hundred reps, add a one pound weight and work back up to one hundred reps. Continue adding one-pound weights until you can do one hundred reps with five pounds. You are now ready to start training again.

Mindful Floor Kicks

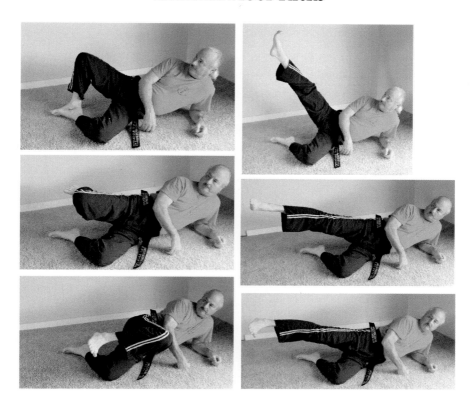

A week or so after ACL reconstruction surgery, you begin rehabilitation exercises at a rehab clinic. After four to six weeks at the clinic, it is time to begin your personal program. Six weeks of clinic rehab may be enough for sedentary living, but not for a competitive martial artist. My personal aim was to strengthen, condition and train that injured knee to make it stronger and more capable than my good knee. I would do four basic kicks - front kick, round kick, hook kick and side kick.

To begin, lie on the floor on your non-injured side. Lift your rehab leg and chamber for a front kick. Then, with your attention focused on the technique, slowly extend your leg into a front kick with your knee locked out. Be sure that the toes are retracted and the ball of your foot is perfectly pointed at an imaginary target. Visualize the ball of your foot striking a board and sense the breaking of the board. Work your way up to ten repetitions. Then, roll over and repeat this mindful exercise on your good leg. *Remember, always strive to combine the necessary and the useful.* After completing this exercise with a front kick, go back to your rehab knee and repeat this exercise with a round, kick, a side kick and a hook kick.

Science has proven that the mental energy of focusing on a specific body part will gradually, over time, increase the blood flow to that area. It also has direct effects at the cellular level. It actually messages your DNA to unwind and make proteins necessary to *upregulate gene expressions to heal the body part.* Do these mindful kicks for forty days. The level of being of the connections between your mind and your kicks will be elevated.

Taping for Dropped Metatarsals

Take two Dr. Scholl's Mole Foam Pads (UPC 14900) and cut them to the form of the ball of your foot. Cut one a bit smaller and overlap them at the metatarsal heads. Peel the cover off the sticky side of the small pad and stick to the top of the larger pad. Then stick the larger pad on to the foot so that the smaller pad is facing out. This covers your metatarsals with a double pad, yet allows the toes to flex fully. Cut two lengths of regular sports tape, one longer than the other, then split them down the middle to form four strips (two about six inches long and two about four inches). Wrap every toe except the pinky toe with a strip, anchoring them on the end of the pad.

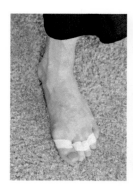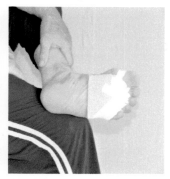

Cut a full strip and seal the outer edge of the pad to the foot, so that the floor cannot cause it to peel back if the foot slides sideways.

 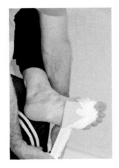 

Next, affix tape under the pad in a diagonal direction. Wrap it over the top of the foot and continue underneath and over the end of the pad to seal it to the bottom of the foot.

 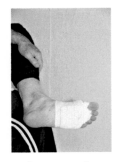 

Continue wrapping in a horizontal manner, overlapping each wrap to secure all parts of the pad to the foot.

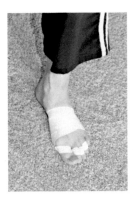

This technique provides a secure pad underneath the heads of the metatarsals. It allowed me to compete in martial art for over five years, until I retired from competition.

Taping for Plantar Fasciitis

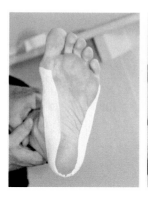 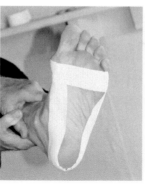 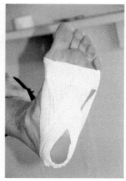

Affix a full strip of sports tape around the perimeter of your foot. Then bring a small strip across your metatarsal heads on the ball of your foot. Next, pull a strip from the head of the big metatarsal down to the heel, moving diagonally across the foot. Wrap the strip around the heel and bring it up again to your small metatarsal. You may add more strips in this way to increase the support. This creates a teardrop shape that covers the plantar fascia where it inserts into the heel.

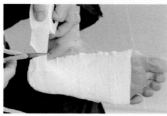

Then tape across the foot with strips of tape. Finally, wrap the perimeter of the foot with sports tape again, to secure the ends of the strips to the first tape you placed down. This creates a solid covering of the entire bottom of the foot.

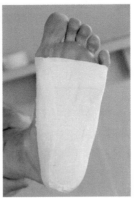

Now you have a solid "cradle" that spreads the force on your heel over the whole area of your foot, reducing the stress on your heel. This taping method enabled me to train with less pain and stand all day while working in the pharmacy.

Stretches for Plantar Fasciitis

Remember that the basic causes of Plantar Fasciitis is two-fold. The first cause of Plantar Fasciitis is a "tight" plantar fascia. The second cause is stress placed upon the fascia because of activity that is beyond normal exertion (in particular, jumping on hard surfaces). In the first cause, you can prevent the condition by stretching and strengthening of the fascia by stretching. You can recover and prevent further problems also by stretching and strengthening of the plantar fascia. The basic stretch is Wall Stretches. Place your hands against the wall and step back into a front stance. Try to put your back heel on the ground and hold for the count of ten. Relax and repeat for two more repetitions. Repeat on good foot for prevention. Do three sets three times daily. Again, forty days is the time you should do them for a discernable result. Once recovery is underway, Upward and Downward Dogs provide an intermediate exercise to stretch and strengthen them further. The most stressful and final exercise is leaning back on the balls of the foot while your knees on the ground. If you can do these, you can probably return to normal training without injury. Remember, three cycles of forty days is required for complete recovery.

My Master Said To Me

One day, during a particularly difficult time of my life,

My Master said to me.

"Always strive to combine the necessary and the useful.

Many times through the duration of your life,

you will find yourself in a difficult situation that you cannot extricate yourself from.

Do not despair.

Simply view it as it is, a necessary condition that you must flow through.

Accept it.

At the same time, try to find something that you can do in this state that will be useful in your striving to grow as a human being.

For you see that if you look at life in this way there will be no negativity.

Nor will you become so completely entangled in the condition that binds you.

You will realize a profit in any situation.

It can be so simple, like being in one room and seeing an object there that belongs in the next room that you are about to enter.

Take it with you and you can double the output of the your work,

and begin to unbind the influences that control your life,

simply by being aware.

Look for the need, which is always there in every situation, and respond to it.

Do not do too much or too little, but what exactly is required.

It is a long process.

This is the same way you work on yourself,

in order to grow as a human being.

Because of your efforts, you hope that someday, you will become able to set your life free."

Chapter 5

Do.
A man is a being that does.
That is a man.
It is not one who thinks, or feels, or cries Lord, Lord,
but one who does.
It is he who makes what he knows into a reality of doing.
Then a man experiences his being.

W. A. NYLAND

THE LAW OF EFFORT

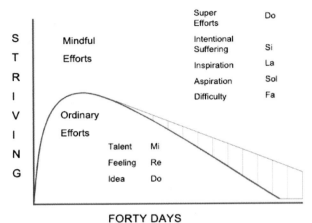

FORTY DAYS

THE FA BRIDGE

The point of difficulty

The place where you want
to stop

When you forget your aim

The Law of Effort

The universe was created and is maintained according to certain laws. Every independent cosmic concentration was created, and now exists, develops, evolves and involves as a result of these laws. The two great laws that pervade all cosmic reality, from the atom to the galaxies, are the Law of Three Forces (The Trinity) and the Law of Seven (Law of Octaves). No matter where any independent cosmic concentration is in the universe, no matter its size or composition, it has *three forces acting through it*. These forces are called the active force, passive force and neutralizing force. For example, the fundamental makeup of the atom has a positively charged proton, a negatively charged electron and a particle with no charge, called a neutron.

Another example of the three main forces are - gravity, electricity and magnetism. Although they are invisible, we see the results of their force. In a human being, The Law of Three manifests as the brain, the body and the feelings. The Yin Yang symbol is the eastern acknowledgement of these forces. Although we can easily see the active and passive (positive and negative) forces, it is difficult for us to recognize the neutralizing (reconciling) force. Yet intuitively we know that if we only have two forces, the stronger or dominant force will always annihilate the weaker force. Therefore, in order for any individuality to exist, the neutralizing or reconciling force must be present for the other two forces to exist in harmony. In humans for example, the triad could be the brain (the totality of intellectual functions) that is the positive force, the body (the totality of physiological, instinctive and physical functions) that is the negative force and the feeling center (the totality of feeling and emotions or motive force) is the neutralizing or harmonizing force. The assignment of positive, negative and neutralizing forces for the centers is only for illustration. Respectively, each center could be positive, negative or neutralizing according to the forces that are conducted through it at any given moment.

The second great law is the Law of Seven, or the Law of Octaves. The Law of Octaves is the form or progression by which the triad of all cosmic wholes evolves and involves (develops and deteriorates). Again, if we take an atom as an example, (and the development of all atomic elements) a fully completed atom is stable when there is a harmonic ratio between the number of electrons in the seven energy levels or electron shells surrounding the nucleus. These shells are matched with an equivalent number of protons in the nucleus. This "marriage" is mediated by a harmonic number of neutrons. This particular arrangement produces an element that cannot be acted upon or changed by outside influences on that level of energy. Its octave is fully completed and becomes the Do for the development of another octave on a higher level. The development of an octave of anything is not a linear or a smooth process, but a combination of processes that appear to be up and down, flowing from one place to another, reciprocating upon itself, influences from the outside mixing in, forming a crescendo, reaching a plateau, and then spilling over to another level and starting a new process. The best way to understand the law of octaves is to study the piano. The keyboard shows seven white keys, with a black key between each one except in two places - between Mi and Fa and between Si and Do. These are called intervals. Each white key and corresponding black key is a complete tone (has a complete octave in the note). However, the two intervals with no black key act as retarding points for any note struck below. This arrangement will show that any tone struck on a white key will develop up the octave until it meets the half tone, beyond which it cannot pass. Force or energy from outside the octave must come in to allow the octave to proceed across the interval. This is why there are no straight lines in Mother Nature. The Law of Octaves is visible in all expressions of Mother Nature. It is displayed in the Solar System, all life forms on earth, plant, animal and man. It is found in the branches of plants and trees, in body and appendages of animals and man. It is visible in the branching of our circulatory system and our nervous system. The sense organs have been formed to take in impressions from the Law of Octaves – the colors seen, the sounds heard and the sensations of touch, taste and smell.

It is not the aim of this chapter to explain the Trinity or Law of Octaves to you. However, until you understand how it manifests inside you, you will never grasp the quality and quantity of effort you must expend to reach a level of excellence in martial art. You can train for years and not reach a higher state of being. You can become depressed and lose your motivation at the very point where you are about to elevate to another level. Check the references and study, study well.

If you want to see your life objectively, study the diagram of the law of effort. Mechanically speaking, all physiological, emotional and intellectual processes begin at birth and rise dramatically during the first twenty to twenty-five years where they peak. The body is fully formed, the feelings are half-formed and the intellect is maybe ten percent formed. The energy that is given to you every day flows through you, and has developed into what you consider to be you. In the ignorance of ego, you claim it, although the truth is that it is given as a gift to you every moment. It is only when your octave of life begins to involve or deteriorate, and you cannot do the things you used to, is when you realize that the same laws which permitted your growth are now active in causing your deterioration or "aging."

All we have talked about so far is mechanical growth and aging, or the force that is given to you by Mother Nature. However, there is another type of force that is not given, yet can be aroused and applied to your life physically, emotionally and intellectually. It is that neutralizing or harmonizing force that can create and produce a totally new and powerful type of energy that can transform your ordinary life. This energy is called "conscious effort." It is a different kind of force. It is the energy of transformation, and it produces a fundamentally different kind of result. It can be called a "higher energy." This elevated aliveness is important to you as a senior practitioner of martial art. This motive drive is present when a person has acquired a goal or an "aim" that is of major importance in their life and is very difficult to achieve. It is a lifelong aim. This kind of energy can arrest involution and create and maintain a new evolutionary process that will lead to the growth of your "being." Being is the totality of who and what you are at any given moment. Being is the capacity to do. *The growth of your being is the great potential of a human being, beyond what Mother Nature has given.* It can be described as the growth of your "individuality," for the being formed is a direct result of your conscious efforts and "intentional suffering." Intentional suffering is defined as making conscious efforts toward a lifelong aim. Understanding conscious efforts and intentional suffering will allow you to grasp the essence of the words we use like spirit, courtesy, respect, loyalty, perseverance, integrity, self-control and will.

What is the difference between mechanical effort and an effort that is conscious in martial art? When we practice martial art, we go to class as prescribed by our instructor and follow his teaching. This is mechanical effort, for we only practice in class, where the instructor's energy stimulates and motivates us. We make no effort apart or beyond what is necessary to complete the class. We are literally being pulled along by the efforts of the instructor.

Conscious effort is when we acquire an aim in martial art that is beyond the classroom experience. Then we practice on our own to work toward that aim that is ours alone.

Elements of Mechanical Effort

No personal aim.

Giving only what is required.

Wanting to stop when things are difficult or suffering begins.

Relying on one's talent only.

Laziness.

Readily diverted by external forces.

Self-calming.

Willingness to quit.

Lack of motivation.

Poor quality and quantity of work.

Elements of Conscious Effort

Directed attention.

Acquisition of an aim.

Giving effort beyond what is necessary toward that aim.

Intentional suffering toward your aim.

Realization of the limitations of your talents, and the willingness to grow beyond them.

Seeing your weaknesses and struggling to eradicate them.

Focusing on your aim every day and eliminating the obstacles in your way.

The joy of conscious exertion.

Aspiration and inspiration.

Application of the appropriate quality and quantity of work necessary for your aim.

An Example of Mechanical Effort

Suppose you have been a martial art practitioner for several years. You have a black belt and are working on your next belt. You feel pretty good about yourself and your accomplishments. Then you look at those who compete in tournaments and you see how good they are, especially if they are in the Top Ten. Or maybe you even have a World Champion in your school. You decide you want to be a World Champion. You say to yourself, this is your aim. Let us formulate this aim as an Octave, exactly represented by the keyboard on a piano.

Do * Re * Mi - Fa * Sol * La * Si - DO

The first Do represents the formulation of your aim to be World Champion, and is the tone struck on the first white key of the piano. The DO represents the accomplishment of your aim - achieving the title of World Champion. The * represent the black keys of the piano. They are the half-tones between the white keys or major tones. The striking of the Do of your aim is translated into your training, by maybe going to an extra class during the week, getting the instructor to correct your form, learning the tournament rules or having a strategy. If the tone of the Do is really strong, maybe you even start training early in preparation. All of this effort brings visions in your mind of the glory and notoriety you will enjoy in your school by winning. In your smugness you have already become a winner.

Then you go to a tournament and fail miserably, you don't even place in forms and you may get knocked out of sparring in the first or second round. Disappointed and disillusioned, you blame the judges for their decisions. They just didn't see the points you scored. You blame your instructor for not training you better. You use all kinds of *self-justification* to explain your failure. You waver in your aim to be World Champion because you realize more is needed than simply striking the first Do of the octave. At this point, you can do two things. You can continue on the way you have always done things, making ordinary efforts and making excuses, not knowing what it really takes and not having the necessary skills, knowledge and understanding to compete at the level of the Top Ten. This is the point on the octave between Mi and Fa, where there are no black keys to carry the original impetus of the Do you struck. It is called the "Fa Bridge." Bruce Lee called this point in your training a "plateau." However in reality, it is the law-conformable retarding point of the octave. It is here that the vibrations are retarded and it is impossible to cross the Fa Bridge with regular or mechanical efforts. Your goal is thwarted. It is the "Point of Difficulty." The other option is to realize that a different kind of effort is needed, that another force must come from outside to pass the Fa Bridge.

Conscious Effort

This is the point where "active mentation" is necessary. Active mentation is directed thought toward a real aim. Active mentation asks the question, "*What does it really take to become a World Champion?*" Active mentation asks what is missing. Where are your weak points? Are your techniques correct, is your attitude right, are you fast enough, are you flexible enough, is your timing, rhythm and movement, memorization, power and balance sufficient for the goal you have set? Finally, are all your techniques automatic, or do you still have to think about them? In short, you must try to look at yourself from all sides, from an objective point of view.

When you do this, another note is struck at Mi on the octave - the mental note. This note brings new knowledge. This can come in the form of reading, watching videos of other fighters and yourself, seeking advice from your instructor, asking a master or *watching those people who are World Champions to see what makes them what they are.*

After this active mentation, you decide that you have good techniques, but you are not fast enough to counter the speed of your opponents. You read a book on plyometric training that promises to develop speed and explosiveness. A light bulb goes off in your head. *I must develop my explosiveness.* You make out a plan for five or six training exercises that mimic the martial art moves you will use to develop the fast twitch fibers and nervous innervation that will increase your speed. You have heard that you must do this training two to three times a week for six weeks before your speed becomes measurably faster. You vow to adhere to the aim you have set for yourself, to practice without fail. You give to yourself an "essence oath" that you will renew your efforts toward the aim you have set for yourself. When you do this, *you engage your conscience*, the motive force of your life. You strike the note Re on the scale of the octave. Your conscience will make your body move, train and make efforts toward your aim.

In this triad, new knowledge Mi, which engages your conscience Re, moves your body Do to strike a new chord. If the vibrations of each note are in harmony with each other, an *overtone* is created that has the quantity and quality of energy necessary to pass the point of difficulty, the Fa bridge in the scale, where there is no black key to give automatic passage. You practice without fail for forty days.

Then you go to a tournament and you get second place! You beat all but the reigning World Champion. Now you *understand* what your training can mean for you. You have reached another level! That level has combined the high (your wish) with the low (the inertia of the body) to produce a medium (a higher level of being), a greater capability and a real change. This higher level of being stimulates your wish to give more effort, to seek more knowledge and to train qualitatively and quantitatively better. This is the triad of effort - new knowledge, commitment to aim and the *delight of movement* that produces understanding. *Understanding is a higher level of being.* Now, since you have made sustained efforts over the span of forty days, something interesting and unique happens to the body. It becomes the active force. It expects to train, it yearns to train. The unified effort of all three parts of yourself has transferred the aim of the mind into the memory of the body. The body's memory does not fail, it does not forget. Connections have been formed between the mind, the body and the feelings. These connections form a harmony that increases the rate of vibrations of each center, therefore vivifying or creating overtones from the unification of the centers. The overtones cross the Fa Bridge and advance to the Sol, La, Si of the octave that represents your striving. Your force grows, a finer vibration is created in your three centers and your level of being has fundamentally changed.

With the body now as the active force, it stimulates the feelings or wish, which engages the mind to learn more. This new triad marches through the next forty days, creating another harmonic unity that tries to overcome the next obstacle, the Si-Do interval, or the last barrier to the fulfilment of the octave. This Si-Do interval is a very difficult barrier, perhaps even more formidable than the Fa Bridge. This is because of two major factors. The first is that the rate of vibrations necessary to cross this interval become higher as the Sol-La-Si of the octave ascends. The second is that the triad formed, body, wish and mind usually does not create the high rate of vibration necessary to form the overtones that will bridge the Si-Do interval. Another triad is necessary. *This triad is special. It is formed from the emotional center not to give up and to achieve the goal no matter what the cost. It is the willingness to sacrifice everything, for the body to overcome all of its pain, injuries and laziness. It is the one pointed focus of the mind to exclude all distractions and generate a mental power that provides a clarity of purpose.*

Another way to understand the three triads is to visualize three dynamic lines of force moving through time. Each line represents one of the three parts or centers of a man - the physical or moving center, the feeling or motive center and the intellectual center or mind.

Moving ----------------->

Feeling------------------>

Intellect----------------->

When trying to ascend the octave, each force acts like a piston in a three-cylinder rotary engine. Each center must apply its force in harmony with the other two cylinders to produce the power needed to pass the Fa Bridge difficulty. If you visualized the forces as they came toward you, it would appear to be a series of triangles in rotation as each active force thrusts forward in a circle.

A third way to understand the effort required to pass the Fa Bridge and the levels of energy formed by the ascension of the octave, we will plot a two-dimensional graph. The vertical axis represents the energy level of effort exerted to develop the octave. The horizontal axis represents the relative progression of your path toward the achievement of your goal.

The amount of energy needed to ascend the octave is represented by a diagonal through the Do Re Mi of the beginning of the octave. This means that there is a one-to-one or geometric relationship between the energy expended and the development of the notes of the octave. However, as the line approaches the Fa Bridge or the interval, the character of the line of energy changes into an exponential function. This means that an increasing amount of energy expenditure is required to produce a diminishing growth of the octave or the level of being. There is a fundamental change in the quality and quantity of energy needed to continue to pursue your goal. This is what is required by a man seeking a high aim.

Super Efforts

No discussion of the Law of Effort is complete without speaking about *super efforts*. To begin with, a super effort is similar to the familiar axiom, "first on the practice field, last off the practice field." People who are very motivated (the emotional triad) to succeed raise their work ethic to spend more time and effort toward their aim than their peers do. Although this is a good beginning for someone unfamiliar with the Law of Effort, there is much more to it than that. Again, the Fa Bridge makes itself apparent *when you want to stop or quit.*

Suppose a man has to walk several miles to get home. It is dark and cold and raining, but he knows shelter and rest are waiting for him. There it is warm and dry and dinner is ready. When he arrives home however, instead of staying he gets up and walks another mile. This is a super effort. The first effort is for a reward, the second effort for one's self. Now suppose he arrives again at home. Instead of sitting down to eat, he goes back outside and does all his chores. What does this kind of effort mean? It is for a purpose. There is an ancient aphorism that will help you understand.

"Always, in every undertaking, perform each task three times. First perform it mechanically for reward, secondly perform it for yourself, and thirdly perform it for a purpose."

This is the meaning of the change in character of the line of effort in the Law of Effort diagram.

How do you apply this to your training? Most people just go to class and do not practice beyond that. This is the Do Re Mi of the beginning of the octave. This is the average taekwondo practitioner - average effort, average results. They expect to go to tournaments and do well, but they are delusional. The student with an aim realizes this is not enough, and he begins to practice on his own. He takes direction from his instructor about what he needs to work on, usually one of the ten attributes. After a period of time, he goes to a tournament and does better but does not achieve the results he desires. He realizes something is missing. He is not fast enough, he does not have enough power, his balance is lacking, his techniques do not have a beginning and ending point, his footwork is poor or his targeting, blocking and hand techniques are not developed. In short, he must work on his weaknesses. Again, an ancient aphorism states - *always struggle with your weaknesses and maintain your strengths.*

The super effort can take place along two general lines - quality and quantity. The quantity of efforts is relatively straightforward - the more repetitions you do and the closer the interval is between repetitions, the higher result. After class or at home, isolate all of your kicking and striking techniques and do ten repetitions of each. Develop automatic movements without thought. Develop your athleticism. Break down all of your techniques to their elemental parts and practice each part. Taekwondo is extremely physically demanding, and you must work on your athleticism.

The second line of a super effort is the development of mindfulness. Mindfulness is bringing the attention of the mind upon the manifestations of the body, or the engagement of two centers at the moment of now. You must introduce mindfulness in your training. This is where the quality of your efforts are important. Sparring is based on several physical attributes that need to be developed to be a high-ranking competitor. Speed, explosiveness, footwork and targeting have be developed individually to raise the level of being of your sparring. Your knowledge of the strength and weakness of each technique must be analyzed, and counter techniques must be developed for each one. This is called mindfulness. You must understand rhythm. Each fighter has a rhythm, and you need to get inside your opponent's rhythm and disrupt it. This is mindfulness. Each move must be choreographed like form practice, so that you do not have to think about any move, but just react. This is mindfulness. You must develop your willingness to commit. This is mindfulness. Most important of all, you need to develop the "sparring mind," to clear it of thoughts, and open up and become aware. *This is the letting go of mindfulness.*

The same goes for form and weapons. Develop all the basics which create the foundation of the activity, then put them all together.

Now you can begin to ponder what a super effort can be.

THE LAW OF EFFORT

ACHEIVEMENT OF GOAL

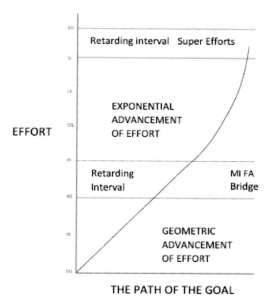

THE PATH OF THE GOAL

The Law of Effort unfolds according the Law of Octaves, like all other phenomena that grow and deteriorate. When the first DO (or goal) is sounded, usually an idea, efforts flow toward the manifestation of that idea. The impetus of that Do ascends the octave to MI in a geometric relationship to the effort expended. A given amount of effort will produce an equal amount of advancement toward the goal. However, the interval between MI and FA retards this progress and the geometric effort does not have enough force to cross. It is here where a major difficulty arises - the disappointment of quitting. Here a man forgets his aim. It is here he is tested. Here he either quits or forms an inner harmony to continue his striving. Renewed efforts of even greater quantity and quality are required to pass this interval – called the MI FA Bridge. Likewise, at the end of the octave, the SI DO interval, even more work is needed to cross it and achieve the goal. The effort to cross SI DO is called a *super effort*.

Chapter 6

*The area of your work
is a reflection of
your inner state.*

Acceleration

Acceleration is a mandatory and integral part of point sparring in tae-kwondo. The definition of acceleration is the constant increase of speed over a period of time squared (multiplied by itself). Gravity is a good example of acceleration. If you were to jump off a tall building, you would fall at 16 feet per second. At the end of two seconds, you would fall at thirty two feet per second and at three seconds, sixty four feet per second, etc. In other words, you would constantly increase speed (accelerate) until you hit the ground, except for wind resistance.

A more relevant example would be a rifle with a cartridge in the chamber and a barrel as long as your leg. When you decide to strike, the firing pin punctures the primer in the cartridge, and an explosion takes place as the powder is ignited. This creates tremendous pressure as the bullet accelerates through the length of the barrel (your kick). The total amount of power generated by this kick is transmitted from the ground, through your muscles, tendons, ligaments and joints by the movement of your body to the target. This expression of power is generated from the initial pulse (like the ignition of the cartridge) as a constant increase in speed (acceleration), with relaxation through the end of the movement (kick). This transmission of power from the initial impulse creates a whipping or snapping movement. It is the instantaneous explosion of all the separate parts and qualities of the body into a single action. This is acceleration. Just as the bullet leaving the barrel begins to slow, the kick decelerates at the end of its extension unless a target is engaged, and then the force is transmitted through it.

The acceleration of the mass (your body, foot or fist) determines how quickly your technique reaches the target. The capability of acceleration depends on many factors. First and foremost is how many fast twitch muscle fibers are involved and the level of preparedness of the supporting neuro-musculature. Second, is the conditioning of the fast twitch fibers, their level of development and the extent of their readiness. All of these qualities express the refinement of their ability for a particular technique. Third is the harmony of all the body parts moving together. Think of it this way. If you just do a punch, it may be clocked at forty miles per hour. If you turn your torso into the punch at the same moment of the punch you would add ten miles per hour to the technique. If you had your knees bent and sprang forward at the same instant you would add ten more miles per hour. So the harmonizing of each body part acting together would produce a punch going sixty miles per hour! Think about it.

All of these influences can be modified to elevate the level of your striving toward competition sparring. This is done by conscious efforts over a long period of time toward the recruitment, development and maturation of your fast twitch muscle fibers. Developing your acceleration will fundamentally elevate your level of sparring.

Acceleration Drills

Stand within kicking distance of a heavy bag in your normal sparring stance. Now bring your front foot back so that it is together with your back foot. Be sure to position yourself exactly, close enough to the bag so that you can strike it one inch deep with full extension of your side kick. Bend your knees so that you are ready to *spring into action* with your hands in guard position. Spring *upward and outward* from this position with both legs. As you are elevating, simultaneously lift your front leg upward and through the side kick chamber and thrust out toward the target. As you lift your kicking leg to the chamber, the upward thrust of the spring will allow your weight to be lifted off the solid sole of your plant foot onto the ball of your foot. This action allows your plant foot to pivot on the ball of your foot and be pulled into the proper hip configuration by the side kick extension. In the same instant that your heel and sole are planted, the kicking foot should be striking the heavy bag or person. All of these different parts of the technique should happen at the same time. Be sure your hands are in guard position before and after the technique. This is important. It puts the emphasis on the kicking technique. Most people lose attention of their hands, dropping or swinging them backward while kicking, thus unconsciously "watering down" the technique. You should strive to devote *every aspect of your effort* to the instantaneous strike of the bag with no "energy leaks." *If you let your hands down or move them backward, they will create a counter force that will slow your acceleration and cause hesitation in your execution.*

Every single fiber of your being should be put into this kick. You must learn how to commit all of you! Do not hold back. Try for maximum acceleration - this is the goal. *POW!* Everything happens in a single instant. Make no telegraphing movements - focus with all of you.

After the strike, re-chamber and hold your balance for an instant. This is important. Most people lose their attention after the kick and lower their leg, opening them up to a counter move. By re-chambering, it keeps your kick under control, protects you from a counter strike and allows you to be in position for a double or triple kick. In fact, the advance drills for acceleration are double and triple kicks. Break down this drill, practice each aspect by itself until you grasp its essence, and then combine them all together into a seamless, instantaneous motion.

Make sure you have done a full warm up before you do acceleration drills, but do the drills before your main workout and before you get fatigued. Remember, you are twenty percent faster when you are warmed up. If you do them when you are fatigued, you will simply train your muscles to be slower. Your main workout should follow these drills.

Do these drills before every sparring session if you can. If you work out on your own, emphasize acceleration in your form and sparring practice. Acceleration drills do not fatigue you, so you should do them at least twice a week. Do all the basic kicks as described with the side-kick. I do number one side kicks, number one round kicks and number one hook kicks, ten repetitions each.

Number two round kicks, reverse side kicks, reverse hook kicks and reverse heel kicks require a slight modification in stance. Instead of your feet being together, spread them out a little wider than a regular sparring stance and keep your knees bent. This enables your rear leg to act like a piston and provide the impulse to launch yourself into number two round kicks and reverse kicks. Understand this.

If I am practicing for a tournament, I would include jump kicks of each kind and then "specialty kicks" afterward.

Make your kicks as perfect as possible in your practice. Remember, the way you practice is the way you will compete. Do these drills two or three times a week for six weeks and you will ascend to a higher level of being in taekwondo in general and especially in your sparring competition. Once you understand the potential for acceleration drills, try to find out how far you can go.

The drills below are the core of your acceleration training.

Kicking Drills

1. #1 Side kick

2. #1 Round kick

3. #1 Hook kick

4. #2 Round kick

5. Reverse side kick

6. Reverse hook kick

7. Reverse heel kick

8. Jump reverse side kick

Upper Body Drills.

Do not ignore your punches and blocks. In tournament sparring, most points are scored with punches. You should practice acceleration drills with your hands as well as with your feet.

Bruce Lee developed a technique called the *Stop Hit*. This technique was used to stop his opponent by a fast kick or punch, before they could even get underway or think about what they were going to do. In order for the *Stop Hit* to be successful, you have to develop your kick or punch to an instantaneous level. The upper body drills described below are taken directly from Bruce Lee's book *The Tao of Jeet Kun Do – The Way of the Intercepting Fist*. I actually discovered his book when I was recovering from a torn ACL. Following the aphorism, *"Always strive to combine the necessary and the useful,"* I realized that while I could not kick, I could practice my hand techniques. After several months of acceleration techniques with my punches, I developed lightning strikes. After I recovered from my knee problem and went back into the ring, I was a well-rounded fighter with few weaknesses. These are the hand technique acceleration drills.

1. Jab

2. Jab-cross

3. Back fist

4. Knife hand strike

5. Ridge hand strike

6. Lean back, outer forearm block-hook punch

7. Keep the bag moving

The Second Level

The second level of the expression of acceleration requires the blending of plyometrics with acceleration drills. This squeezes out of the kicking or punching motion maximum acceleration, explosiveness and execution. Begin hopping or bouncing while you are practicing these acceleration drills. Hopping adds plyometric principles to your efforts and enhances all that you have been training for. You harmonize rhythm, timing, power and speed. Practice all of the drills while hopping. No one can stop you.

Acceleration Kicking Drills

Side Kick

Stand exactly one side kick extension unit away from the bag, this helps with distancing your kicks. Your feet are together with your knees bent into a crouch. This is important because your explosiveness and the emphasis of the kick comes from your powerful leg muscles. Spring your body upward and outward as if you are jumping forward. Then in one motion, shoot out your side kick. As your body elevates, it allows you to pivot your plant leg around on the ball of your foot so that you have a "solid sole" with your heel pointed toward the target at exactly the same moment that your side kick strikes the bag. Retain your balance, immediately pull back into side kick chamber and hold it an instant, ready for another kick. This is important in order to protect yourself if your opponent rushes you. Remember, put every fiber of your being into the kick, POW! Let no part of your body hinder the kick. Do for ten repetitions. Then repeat this technique with number one round kick, number one hook kick and number one hook kick/round kick combination. Then repeat on your opposite leg.

Number Two Round Kick

Begin in an exaggerated sparring stance with knees bent. Push off hard with your back foot like a piston. At the same moment you push off, slightly elevate your front foot to the ball of your foot. This will allow the kick to pull your front foot around as your kicking leg heads toward the target. Lead with your shoulder and let it pull your torso around, which adds tremendous power and speed to your kick like a whipping motion. Strike the bag with everything you have on the top of your foot. Do not allow yourself to come down after the kick, but pull your kicking foot back into a round kick chamber, ready to kick again. Regain your balance for an instant and hold.

Reverse Side Kick

Assume a wide sparring stance with your knees bent. Push off hard with your back leg, using it like a piston. The push off should elevate the heel of your plant leg off the ground onto the ball of your foot, allowing it to pivot around and land as a solid sole at the moment of your strike. The force of the piston should thrust your torso forward into a whirl. Lead with your head and your body will follow. Be sure your side kick chamber is as high as possible so the kick will come straight out. The side kick extension should strike the bag at the exact instant that your plant foot has a solid sole with your heel pointed toward the target. The kick should be one motion, POW! Immediately pull the extension back into a chamber and hold for an instant and regain your balance in case you need to kick again. Repeat the technique again for ten repetitions. Remember, go for maximum acceleration and commit totally to the kick. Always regain your chamber with balance, before you put your foot down.

Reverse Heel Kick

Begin in an exaggerated sparring stance. Push off with your back leg like a piston. At the same instant elevate your front foot to the ball of your foot and thrust your front hip forward. When you push off with your back leg whirl your torso and head around to locate the target. This will pull your kick around powerfully. As your heel strikes the bag, your plant foot will become a solid sole. Do not allow yourself to lose your balance and come down. Instead, regain your balance, rechamber and hold for a moment.

Jump Reverse Side Kick

Begin with your legs shoulder width apart. Drop into a deep knee bend and immediately spring upward with a powerful thrust from both legs. As the body leaps skyward the knees elevate into a side kick chamber and the whole body does a "switch" in direction. At the peak of your leap, the side kick thrust strikes the bag. Immediately withdraw the side kick after the strike and land on both legs, ready to kick again. Repeat this technique five times. Your plyometric training will help you with this technique.

Hand Techniques

Begin crouched with your feet together and knees bent, keeping your hands in sparring guard. Spring upward and forward with all your force. At the same time, strike out hard with a jab. Try to synchronize the jab with the spring from your legs so that all your force is concentrated into the bag. At the end of the jab, you should be balanced on your front leg. Gather yourself to the starting position and repeat ten times. Repeat this exercise with all of your hand techniques, back fist, knife hand strike and ridge hand strike. This is what Bruce Lee called the *Stop Hit*.

The next technique to practice is jab-cross. At the end of the jab, pull the jab back by rotating the jab shoulder backward with force and at the same instant shoot out your cross with all your power and strike the bag. Pulling back the jab shoulder synchronizes the force of your cross to produce a knock out strike. The hips will naturally rotate to end up in cross stance. The time between the jab and the punch should be reduced to a minimum, causing a rhythm of bap-bap sound as you strike the bag. Repeat ten times.

Although it is not a real acceleration technique, this speed drill is of great value. The object is to keep the bag going with alternating back fists. Not only does this increase your punching speed, it also shuts down your mind and allows your body to proceed without influence of the mind. Practice this until failure.

Outer-forearm Block-hook Punch

This last technique is a very important one if you are facing a powerful adversary who can round kick many times before putting their foot down. Stand close to your speed bag to simulate a round kick to your head. In one motion, lean way back while executing an outer-forearm block and stepping away with your back leg. As you step away from the kick, bend your knee to gain force. Then, using your back leg as a powerful piston, spring forward and deliver a hooking punch to the bag. Repeat ten times on both sides.

Chapter 7

*Every type of work
requires its own
quality and quantity
of effort.*

Explosiveness

From Camo to Black Belt, most sparring development is in learning techniques, combinations, strategy and general sparring. This type of learning leads to expanding the sparring envelope of the student, which is now a horizontal type of development. In order to progress beyond this level, all techniques must have some type of vertical component or depth of development. This fundamental change is necessary in order to have consistent success or even some type of excellence in sparring.

Depth or vertical growth of a technique involves physiological changes in the muscles, connective tissue and the nervous system. These changes require a conscious effort over a long period of time. The minimum time for a technique to develop a higher level of execution is about forty days of conscious, specific practice. It takes a long time for the physical body in all of its totality to "reset" on a new level according to the demands placed upon it.

Forty Days and Forty Nights

This biblical reference is so important to understand when it comes to changing your level of being. It is spoken about in detail in the chapter *The Law of Effort*, where the Law of Octaves is discussed. It has been known since antiquity as the period of time necessary for the cycle of any particular phenomenon to arise, grow, deteriorate and end. Physiologically speaking, all the cells of the body "turn over," or are born, mature and die over determinate periods of time. The body is constantly renewing itself. The function of each cell is determined by its "blueprint" or DNA and the "expression" of the genes formed by the DNA. The expression of genes is turned on and off by chemical messengers and reactions to external stimuli. In the case of muscle, connective and neural tissue, it is new training that changes the gene expression and forms new cells commensurate with the new stresses imposed upon them. This period of time is necessary for these changes to take place. Once the sense and significance of forty days and forty nights is understood, the mystery of how long and how much to train is solved.

Recruitment Training

To be successful in taekwondo point sparring, fast techniques are mandatory. Speed, however, is not the proper word to describe the quality of what needs to be developed. More accurately, the correct word is *explosiveness.*

Physiologically speaking, striated muscle tissue is divided into two types of muscle fibers. These fibers are called *slow twitch* (type I) and *fast twitch* (type II). Slow twitch fibers are found in muscle groups that are used by the body when strength and endurance is required. Activities like standing, walking, jogging or lifting weights stimulate the growth and maintenance of slow twitch fibers. Slow twitch fibers fatigue very slowly and can perform many repetitions and sustain long periods of constant contraction without failure. These slow twitch fibers are red in color, tend to contract slowly and work best in aerobic conditions. Generally, slow twitch fibers are found predominantly in the calf, thigh, hip, buttocks-abdomen, back and intercostal muscles. These muscles are always tensed to some degree because of their eternal struggle to keep the body in a vertical position to oppose the force of gravity.

Fast twitch fibers are lighter in color and contract very quickly. Fast twitch fibers provide immediate strength, speed and power. They work mostly in anaerobic conditions, therefore they tend to fatigue quickly. They are stimulated to grow and are recruited into muscle groups responsible for rapid movements and fine motor skills. Muscles of the face, hands and arms are predominately fast twitch fibers, for they perform quick movements and require dexterity of grasping and using tools. Martial art is an example of an activity that needs the recruitment and development of fast twitch fibers.

Each person has their own "mix" of these slow and fast twitch fibers as a result of their genetic inheritance, and to some extent how they live their life. This is why some people are naturally talented in one sport or another. For instance, Michael Jordan was packed with fast twitch fibers, which allowed him to evade, jump, shoot and make baskets with unprecedented success. Arnold Schwarzenegger was probably endowed with a majority of slow twitch fibers, which allowed him to train with weights for hours and reach amazing musculature as a result.

However, in each person there appears to be a quota of muscle fibers that are *uncommitted*. These uncommitted fibers seem to be able to go either way, depending upon the type of training one engages in. They are rarely developed, because typical training does not take into account the specific *quality of effort* necessary to stimulate them to commit. This means that with specific training, these uncommitted fibers can be developed one way or the other. This training is called *Recruitment Training*. In martial art, especially taekwondo point sparring, we want to recruit those uncommitted fibers to become fast twitch fibers. After a long period of time of recruitment training, you will notice that your techniques become explosive. Explosiveness is the blend of power, acceleration and focus. The character of this explosiveness is a *pulse*, which is set in motion by bundles of fast twitch fibers firing at the same time. The more fast twitch fibers you recruit, and the more developed they are in the sense that they contract together, the more instantaneous force can be propelled through your limbs in the form of a kick or strike. As we talked about in the chapter on acceleration, a greater acceleration reflects a greater initial pulse of power. *POW!*

The development of explosiveness requires a conscious effort at the impetus of the movement. This conscious effort has a specific sense of focus. The process of recruitment and harmonic development of groups of fast twitch fibers and the nervous system to ignite them, will be a constant theme in your training if you want to excel in sparring. The drills that follow are plyometric drills that I developed to recruit my fast twitch fibers. Plyometric drills will be extensively treated in a chapter of its own.

1. Alternating lunges with torso twists

2. Walking lunges

3. Box jumps

4. Side kick chamber hops

5. Round kick chamber hops

6. Four point drill

7. Skipping side kicks

8. Skipping round kicks

9. Skipping hook kicks

10. Repeat stationary side kicks

11. Repeat stationary round kicks

12. Repeat stationary hook kicks

13. Practicing Explosiveness

To obtain meaningful results in explosive techniques will require intentional practice over a long period of time. The degree of development is governed by certain influences. These influences are called *The Law of Effort*. This law describes the influences, stages of growth, retarding factors and the quality and quantity of effort needed to achieve and maintain a particular level of explosiveness. This law has been elucidated in a previous chapter.

At least one workout period a week devoted exclusively to these drills for a period of about six weeks (forty days) is required to change the threshold of your explosiveness. There are three reasons for this. First, it takes this effort over this time to recruit a portion of uncommitted fast twitch fibers. Second, it takes this effort and time to refine the nervous regulation needed to control large groups of fast twitch fibers. In other words, the neuromuscular pulse must cause maximum contraction of groups of fibers in the shortest period of time. The third reason is that during this training process, psychological changes must occur that separate the physical manifestation from any mental interference. To allow the body to execute explosiveness without the retardation of any mental or thinking process is a *major shift in consciousness*. This state has many names. In Zen it is called *No Mind*. In the West it is called *The Zone*. In Middle Eastern culture it is known as *Simultaneity*. This shutting down of the mind, opening up awareness, allowing unfettered expression, giving over to the body and letting go, is also known as *Freedom*.

Chapter 8

As long as you command respect,
even fear,
from your peers,
you should keep playing...

Michael Jordan

Plyometric Training

In previous chapters we have explored acceleration and explosiveness. Now we come to the third aspect of the triad called pylometrics. The discovery and exploration of plyometric training is the path that will raise your level of sparring and spill over into all aspects of martial art. Plyometric drills will recruit those fast twitch muscle fibers.

A plyometric movement is one that is preceded by an *eccentric contraction*. An eccentric contraction is one that stretches the muscles, ligaments and tendons until they are under tension. This tension *stores energy* from the pull or force of gravity. This energy is released when the muscles contract and elevate the body off the ground. For example, stand on a box and drop down to the floor. When you land on the floor, the energy from the fall is transferred and stored in the muscles and tendons of your hips, legs, knees, calves, ankles and feet as they contract to cushion the fall. If you do nothing, all of the energy of the fall is dissipated into the floor. If you immediately jump upward after touching the floor, the energy stored from the fall adds to the muscular contraction of the jump that propels you skyward. The contraction of the muscles for the jump is called *concentric contraction*. In between the eccentric contraction and the concentric contraction is a split second when the muscles contract, but there is no movement. It is called *isometric contraction*. This isometric contraction is the impulse of the movement. If you only jumped from the floor, the forces of the jump would be isometric and concentric muscular contraction. To clarify this idea further, see the energy generating equation below.

Standing Jump

Isometric + concentric = *total energy released*

Box Jump

Eccentric + isometric + concentric = *Total Energy Released*

In addition to the synchronized eccentric, isometric and concentric contractions that increase the height of the jump, there is another mechanism activated by the box jump that further increases the energy released to make your jump higher. This is called the *stretch reflex*. The stretch reflex is activated by stretch receptors in your muscles called proprio-receptors.

Proprio-receptors are specialized nerve endings embedded in muscle and tendon tissue that constantly monitor and regulate the stretch of the muscles. The stretch reflex resists the stretch of the muscle as it approaches its maximum length. This is a natural phenomenon that protects the muscles from becoming overstretched to the point of tearing. If these proprio-receptors detect a rapid stretch that might damage the tissues involved, they send signals to your nervous system to contract these muscles to stop the stretch and prevent damage. When you add the stretch reflex to the energy equation, it looks like this.

Eccentric + Stretch Reflex + Isometric + Concentric =
TOTAL ENERGY RELEASED

As you can see, the harmonic movement in a plyometric jump releases far more energy than a stationary jump and is much more instantaneous. This results in an explosive movement. All these big words and explanations are used to describe a very simple activity. Once the sense and significance of this activity is understood, the totality of the movement can be summarized. *Stay on the ground for the least amount of time possible!*

Plyometric training is similar to any other in order to achieve measurable results. It must be practiced regularly for a period of about six weeks before meaningful gains will be noticed. Plyometrics put tremendous stresses on your muscles, tendons, ligaments and joints. At least a full day of rest is necessary after a plyometric workout. Be sure you do a full warmup before engaging in a plyometric workout or you may injure yourself. Start off with a single set of each technique. Every six weeks, increase by one set, until you are doing three sets of each technique. Once you can do three sets of each drill to failure, you will be an animal! Select plyometric drills that mimic the techniques you will be doing in taekwondo.

The most important point in plyometric training is to *do each technique until failure.* In other words, do each technique until you cannot do it anymore. *This is what recruits, develops and maintains fast twitch fibers!*

Below are listed the plyometric drills I practiced on a weekly basis when I was competing. I devoted one day each week just to these plyometric drills. After experimenting with them, incorporate the ones that have value for you into your training. Commit yourself to plyometrics and watch your sparring explode!

1. Alternating lunges with torso twist

2. Walking lunges

3. Box jumps

4. Double Knee Slap Leaps

5. Four point drill

6. Side kick chamber hops

7. Round kick chamber hops

8. Side kick hops

9. Round kick hops

10. Hook kick hops

The Practice of Plyometrics in Sparring

The simplest plyometric activity one can do is hopping, skipping or bouncing when you are sparring. This movement has many beneficial effects on your sparring. First, it engages your opponent's visual sense (flicker-fusion) with constant movement. Since your opponent cannot fixate on your target area or appendages, it slows down his reaction time to any technique you initiate. Second, if your opponent is flat-footed, you can take up to four bounces for each step he takes if he does not hop. This allows you to react four times quicker when it comes to positioning, evading or kicking. It also allows you to *get inside of his rhythm and break his rhythm.* Third, it allows you to do a technique off of each hop. Fourth, each technique will have explosive power to it.

The most interesting and most important secret of hopping is that it shuts down your subjective mind, or the thinking process. The subjective mind is like a machine that has been set in motion and mechanically runs without conscious effort. It is always anticipating the future and remembering the past. It is also engaged in internal dialogue (inner conversations) and imaginings. The worst thing about subjective mind, sometimes called the "formulating apparatus," is that it constantly identifies with the visual experience. The reason for this is how we see. The visual event is focused in the eye on the fovea centralis and is sent to the brain for interpretation, where it literally swims around in the subjective process until an impulse of reaction is initiated. We are constantly refocusing on points of interest and do not take into account the totality of *seeing everything that is in front of us*. This constant refocusing is the driving force for the identification of the mind on objects. This identification process slows down reaction time in sparring. It is never now. This subjective mental process has a certain speed or rhythm associated with it. It basically runs on a two-count or in some real intellectuals, a four-count. This is how long it takes to formulate a thought or action. This thought process is fine for most of ordinary life, but in the ring it is a tremendous hindrance, for it tries to do the work of the moving center, which is thirty thousand times faster.

The speed of the body is thirty thousand times faster than subjective thought when trained to *act without thought*. Therefore, shutting down the thought process allows movement without hindrance and awareness without thought. Your vision changes also to the peripheral vision that can recognize movement, direction, intent and can take in impressions which are inaccessible to your intellect. This is a fundamentally different state of being. *This is the Sparring Mind. The Sparring Mind is now.* The more and more you enter the Sparring Mind, and the longer you stay in it, the more and more you will be able to manifest within it. This is living in the now - being able to direct the body without hindrance and responding exactly to the need that is present - not too much or too little, but *exactly what is required*. This doing, while experiencing your being, is called *Waking Up! The person most awake will always be the better!*

Hopping will accelerate your body movement to an eight count or even a sixteenth count. The subjective mind cannot keep up and will shut down. You will begin to open up. You need to reach an eight count to spar effectively. You need a sixteenth count to win consistently.

The waking up in sparring will be the subject of an entire chapter called *The Sparring Mind (Simultaneity).*

Integrating Plyometric Training into Your Workout

When I was training for competition, there was so much to do that time became a real factor in my efforts. I consistently competed in forms, sparring, weapons and combat weapons. The technical challenges for each type of competition were considerable, and the bulk of my time was spent maintaining a high level of refinement of technique. This left little time for new athletic development or plyometric training.

After considerable experimentation, I developed a once-a-week workout that combined many different facets of training. I found that plyometrics complemented any workout. With this in mind, I developed a *total-kick-butt-workout*. This workout was "affectionately" called Mr. K's Kick-Butt workout by my students. Well, maybe I should leave out the word affectionate. It incorporated all my training needs into a synergistic workout once a week. It lasted a little over an hour. The components of this workout are listed below. It is important to do these elements in the exact order that are listed.

1. Dynamic warm up

2. Acceleration drills

3. Choreography

4. Sparring

5. Plyometrics

6. Anaerobic kicking

7. Passive stretching

I found that this workout would maintain the level of being necessary to win consistently.

There is a definite story behind my plyometric training and how it became the precipitating factor in my success in the ring.

After the World Championships in 1998, I was at a very low point. I had trained hard for six months and was defeated in the second round of sparring. I did not even place in forms. I went to class regularly and did everything I was told, but I felt there was something missing from my training that was not available in my taekwondo classes. I knew I had fair flexibility and good techniques, but it seemed that I was not quick enough. I was exhausted after tournaments.

That summer, I went to Rifle, Colorado to visit my best friend. While I was there, we went to a barber shop to get a haircut. As I waited my turn, I picked up a magazine called *Outside*. While perusing the articles, I found a section called *Bodywork*. Underneath the title was a caution – *This, in Fact,*

Will hurt a Bit. It showed several plyometric exercises that promised to increase speed, jumping ability and quickness in other sports. In addition, there were other exercises that would develop the *stabilizer muscles* of the ribcage, back, abdomen and hips.

Immediately, I knew I had found what I was looking for. The barber let me have the magazine, and I read it several times on our way back to Texas. I ordered a subscription to the magazine and some back issues. I also read a book called *Jumping Into Plyometrics* by Donald A. Chu. After considerable research, I began to experiment as to which exercises would benefit me in my taekwondo training. At the same time I was reading Bill Wallace's book *Dynamic Stretching and Kicking* and a book by Thomas Kurtz called *Stretching Scientifically: A Guide to Flexibility Training.* By the fall, I had developed a training program that was designed to increase my flexibility, quickness, jumping ability, endurance and stabilizer muscles. As my training progressed, it began to recruit the fast twitch muscle fibers needed for the extreme demands of competition sparring.

The workout turned out to be a forty-minute program that I practiced once per week, with two days of rest following it. Because of the extreme demands on my body, I actually cut out one of my taekwondo classes and only went to sparring class once a week. To make up for the general class I missed, I trained at home that day, dividing my time between form repetition and choreographing sparring moves on the ball, headache bag and heavy bag. For forms I did each segment three to four times each, and for sparring I practiced each move I planned to use in competition three to four times. I ended up training three times a week - a plyometric workout, a forms/sparring workout and a regular sparring class. I did this for six weeks and then attended a regional tournament in Clear Lake, Texas.

I won my first match 5/0. In my second match, I was bowled over by an aggressive boxer type and injured my knee as he fell on top of me. After a minute or two, I got up and won the match 5/1. In my third match, I was ahead 2/0 when my opponent rushed me. I did a jump reverse sidekick to his jaw for three points. He was six feet tall. Eternal Grand Master H. U. Lee's table was right in front of our ring. A move like this in the 50-60 year old ring was, and still is, unheard of. A whole new world opened in front of me. I understood then what the value of my training held for me. *The fact was that my training was simply beyond that of any of the opponents I faced.*

After that day, I did not lose for three years.

Plyometric Training

Alternating Lunges with Torso Twist

Begin with your arms backward and torso twisted. Step out into a deep lunge and twist your torso while swinging your arms to other side at the same time. Try to twist as far as possible and lunge as deep as possible without putting your knee on the floor. Then push your body up with force. When erect, immediately repeat the lunge and torso twist to the opposite leg and side. Repeat until failure. In addition to its plyometric value, this exercises your stabilizer muscles. These are the oblique, intercostal and lower back muscles. They are the core of all your kicks and punches.

Walking Lunges

Begin erect, then step out into a long, deep lunge. Keep your hands near your abdomen. Then force your body erect. Then immediately step out into another lunge with the opposite leg. Continue across the floor of the dojang until failure. In my opinion, walking lunges are the best exercise for your legs. If you want to make it more stressful, hold a light barbell on your shoulders.

Four Point Drill

Mark off the edges of a square on the floor with pieces of tape. The square should be two or three feet on each edge. Then place a piece of tape in the center of the square. Begin by standing in the middle of the square with your hands on your abdomen for balance. Jump to the left front corner of the square while turning your hips into the jump and land sideways. Immediately jump back to the center of the square. Then jump backward to the back left corner of the square, again twisting your hips in air and landing sideways to the jump. Jump back to the center and continue going around the square counter-clockwise in this manner until all four corners have been hit. This is one cycle. Repeat this cycle until failure. Rest a minute or two. Then repeat the four point drill beginning with the right front corner first and continuing around the square in a clockwise direction. Do until failure. Do not stop until failure. Stay on the ground as little as possible. Be sure to turn the hips toward the point you are jumping to. This will give you the dexterity to land in the proper position for a number one side kick, round kick or hook kick. In my opinion, this drill is extremely important in developing your ability to position yourself for a kick, whether advancing or retreating in sparring. The quickness required in this drill can bring you to an eight count or even a sixteen count, which will shut down your subjective mind and open up your sparring mind. Keep your feet together and your hands on your abdomen to maintain the balance necessary to make your legs do this.

Box Jumps

Build your box 12" high, 18" wide and 24" long. Place one foot on the box with your hands on your abdomen. Jump straight up as high as you can go. Switch feet while in midair and land with the opposite foot on the box. Immediately jump again and continue alternating jumps. Stay on the ground for as short a time as possible. This will allow all of the jump energy to be transferred into the next jump. Look down at the box while jumping to avoid landing awkwardly. Keep your hands close to your abdomen for balance and try to get maximum height from each jump. Do until failure. You should have a sense of yourself in midair without gravity at the top of your jump for a moment.

Double Knee Slap Leaps

Stand erect with your hands at waist level. Gather yourself, bend your knees and jump straight up as high as you can. As you jump, bring your knees up and slap the palms of your hands with them. Land with your knees bent, hands at your waist and repeat the jump until failure. Stay on the ground for as little time as you can. The plyometric idea is to instantly transmit the force of your landing into a new jump. Bringing up the knees increases the height of your jump and will help you with all of your jump kicks. This is a very stressful plyometric drill and could cause plantar fasciitis. Be sure you are warmed up and on a padded floor. I recommend shoes with this drill. At first, you may have to take smaller jumps in between the high jumps to retain your balance.

Side Kick and Round Kick Chamber Hops

Begin with a side kick chamber, your knee in front of your body with hand guard up. Push off with the ground leg and hop forward while trying to retain your chamber. Repeat this hopping down the dojang floor without stopping. Try to retain proper chamber and hand guard. Hop until failure. Rest for a minute or two. Then switch sides and repeat this drill off the other leg. Try to stay on the ground as little as possible. It is not a race to get to the end of the floor. The goal is not to make long hops, but to put the emphasis on a good chamber, good hop, good balance and good hand guard. Repeat this drill with round kick chambers in back of your kicking leg.

Side Kick, Round Kick and Hook Kick Hops

Begin in a side kick chamber with your guard up. Push off from the ground foot while exaggerating chamber. Strike out with a side kick thrust while in midair. After landing, repeat this side kick hop down the floor. Try to stay on the ground for as little time as possible. Repeat until failure. Rest a minute or two, then repeat this drill on the opposite leg. This drill is just like side kick hops, except you add the side kick to each hop. This exercise has a definite rhythm to it in order to continue down the floor without stopping. Try to sense this rhythm and maintain it down the floor. It is not a race to get down the floor. Try to maintain good guard, good hop, good balance, perfect rhythm and good side kick extension. This drill is a very powerful plyometric exercise. Exaggerating your chambers will help with your rhythm and thrusting. There are so many benefits to be obtained from this drill. Repeat this drill with round kicks and then hook kicks.

Chapter 9

Victory loves preparation.

Amat Victoria Curam

Targeting

In order to win sparring matches in competition taekwondo you must be able to score points. To score points you must hit the legal target area. Up until this point in taekwondo, you have been taught safety first and self-control (not hurting people). In your striving to progress further you must now learn to actually strike the target while having self-control. The development of targeting skills requires *intent*. Intent is the motivation to strike the target with a *discriminating effect*. Intent may also described as the focus of the quality of power of the technique into a certain point upon or within your opponent.

If you want to hurt someone then your technique will have a certain quality of power and focus that expresses that intent. It is the same intent you would have in breaking boards. The execution of your strikes, kicks and blocks will bury themselves from two to six inches inside the body of your opponent. This type of intent actually slows down the speed and recovery of your technique because of the *time on* contact and the lack of re-chamber. The power generated by this force may affect your balance and decrease your ability to recover from the technique. It will also increase the time to execute a repeat technique or flow directly into another one.

Since our type of sparring, point sparring, does not require such force in order to score a point, your intent must be modified to that aim. The aim is to touch the target area or penetrate up to one inch. This demands a *different quality of power*. The quality of this power is described as a *pulse*. This means the emphasis of the technique is at the *beginning and then relaxation throughout the extension of the technique*. This creates a whipping or snapping motion. This kind of intent allows you to strike with maximum acceleration and to re-chamber quickly for a repeat strike or to flow seamlessly into another technique or combination. *This is the proper intent we wish to develop in point sparring.*

In order to strike the target every time with the proper intent requires a great deal of practice. Targeting is the harmonization between the perception of sight and the appropriate body response. In ordinary life we practice avoidance of contact. For instance we walk around people on the street so we will not contact them. We also practice this avoidance while driving a car so we will not collide with another vehicle.

Targeting requires the opposite. *You are trying to intercept and cause a collision between your striking technique and your opponent's target area.* You must strive to penetrate the essence of the interception of the target area with the proper intent in order to be successful in point sparring. Some martial art systems even have this in their name, like Bruce Lee's book *Tao of Jeet Kune Do – The Way of the Intercepting Fist.* There is another psychological approach to targeting. It is like being drawn toward a lost love, a wish to be reunite with the target. This type of intent can be a very powerful force.

It is really wonderful to watch people who have ascended to the level of this proper intent in sparring. Instead of a brawl, they make no unnecessary strikes or blocks. Their footwork is constantly putting them in the proper position for a strike. They respond with the proper technique for each situation that is presented. They can spar with any level of opponent and adapt their targeting skills to that level or style and not hurt them. This is truly self-control at a very high level. This is your goal.

To attain this level skill, you must practice a great deal. There are many drills that can help you achieve this. You should practice them at least once a week. These drills can be divided into partner drills and solo drills. Partner drills are done with pork chops. The holder should hold the pork chop high and then drop it unexpectedly. An immediate response is required to blend targeting with timing. Timing is the time between the recognition that the target is exposed and when the technique actually strikes the target. If a body pad is used, it will be held sideways and then quickly turned into a target position. An immediate response is required.

Partner drills with the pork chop or body pad.

1. Number one round kicks

2. Number one hook kicks

3. Skipping round kicks across the floor

4. Skipping hook kicks across the floor

5. Number two round kicks

6. Number two round kicks across the floor

7. Number one side kicks with body pad

8. Reverse side kicks with body pad

9. Step reverse side kicks with body pad

Solo drills with hanging bag, headache bag or hanging ball

1. Number one round kicks

2. Number one hook kicks

3. Number one side kicks

4. Reverse side kicks

5. Reverse hook kicks

6. Number two round kicks

7. Skipping round kicks

8. Skipping hook kicks

9. Skipping side kicks

10. Step reverse side kicks

11. Jump side kicks

12. Jump round kicks

13. Jump hook kicks

When practicing these drills, try them first while standing to practice overcoming the inertia of stillness. Then when you get some proficiency, do them while bouncing to engage the timing of a plyometric explosion. If you are doing these drills with the hanging ball, try to keep the ball going and not let it touch you. The practice of these drills will reduce your reaction time, increase your accuracy and score more points.

My targeting drills were taken from Dana Hee's training video *Taekwondo Drills for Modern Competition Sparring*. Dana Hee was the first U.S. Women's Olympic Champion in taekwondo in 1988. Her drills bring together the concepts of acceleration, explosiveness, plyometrics and targeting. You should get this video.

There is one other thing to practice. *See your target and mark it.* Give your body a sight picture to remember. This is important. While in the ring before each fight, usually my opponent would try to *stare me down.* While he was doing this, I would be scrutinizing his target areas and say to my body, *there it is.* This simple act actually trains the body to strike that particular area. It is giving over to the body the responsibility of hitting the sight picture. It works if you train this way before each kick or punch. This is especially important in reverse kicks, mark your target before you turn, then look for it on the reverse. Practicing like this will synchronize your sight picture with your foot or punch striking the target. You get the sight picture and your body does the rest. Have you ever seen a video of a cheetah chasing a gazelle? His whole body is in full flight but his head and eyes are focused on his prey. Be a predator.

The Territorial Imperative

One of the great laws of organic life on earth is The Territorial Imperative. All living creatures must have a certain space in between them. You can see it everywhere. Birds sitting on a line, spacing between herd animals and the territories of predators. In each species, every individual has its own space around them. When the space between individuals become compressed due to over population or overcrowding, stress and conflict result. When you are in a line to check out at a store, you naturally space yourself according to some instinctive knowledge. If a stranger enters your space without your permission you become uncomfortable and back up or become aggressive and fight. This is your instinctive center, which is part of your moving center, preserving your Territorial Imperative. Generally for a human, it is a sphere around you approximately the same distance as your outstretched arms. In sparring, if you are sensitive enough, you can use this instinctive law to your advantage. In targeting *you must know when your opponent is within striking distance to either withdraw, block, kick or punch.* Your instinct will tell you, and it is amazing how your body will react without thought, when your opponent enters your personal space trying to score a point. Try to train this very valuable instinctive knowledge to distance yourself perfectly to avoid an offensive threat or counter with your own technique. Think about this.

Chapter 10

A man goes to knowledge as he goes to war.
He is wide-awake, with fear, respect,
and absolute assurance.
Going to knowledge or going to war
in any other manner is a mistake.
And whoever makes it may not live
to regret his steps.

Carlos Castaneda
The Teachings of Don Juan
A Yaqui Way of Knowledge

My Style of Sparring

My style of sparring has developed over many years of training and competition. There have been several teachers who have been instrumental in my acquisition of multiple skills. By taking these skills into the ring I fleshed out a skeleton of sparring strategy. This strategy was refined by the men and women whom I trained with and my competitors.

The single most "spiritualizing" factor in my growth has been the *willingness to find out what it really takes to achieve the level of a World Champion.*

My style is centered on four fundamental principles that focus my training in a systematic way.

1. The striving to develop the physical attributes and athleticism of the body to fully master the techniques necessary to compete at the Top Ten level. Competition martial art (taekwondo) is a very demanding endeavor. These techniques require a certain level of athleticism just to do them and a very high level to execute them with effectiveness. Developing the physical body to provide the foundation for the practice of these skills is a constant and ongoing effort. Without this foundation you will never be able to practice the following principles.

2. The wish to practice my basic techniques until they are better than anyone else. Most people practice taekwondo on a horizontal level without penetrating the essence of each individual technique. Therefore their execution never spills over the threshold necessary to excel. Hence they just "play taekwondo." Only when you penetrate the essence of the technique by conscious and conscientious practice will the level of execution attain excellence. This this called vertical or depth of technique. It is extremely difficult to obtain excellence with every technique. Therefore your striving should be to develop your *basic techniques* to a very high level. One of my favorite aphorisms comes from Miyamoto Musashi, Japan's greatest swordsman, "*The more and more you seek the spirit of the thing, the more and more the Spirit of the Thing will reveal itself to you.*" Try to understand this, each technique has depth beyond measure. Generally speaking, at First Degree Black Belt you

should have one *very good technique* to win with regularity. At Second Degree, you should have two really good techniques. At Third Degree you should have three, at Fourth Degree four and Fifth Degree five. The Law of Quintessence.

3. The practice of choreography to harmonize multiple techniques that meet every situation found in the ring. Choreography is the stringing together of several techniques to produce a certain effect. Sparring creates many different situations that must be taken advantage of in order to score. There are an infinite variety of these situations that arise, *but in reality there are several that recur most of the time.* Knowing how to prepare for each situation and choreographing the moves necessary to score in that particular moment is a *level of being all its own.* Without the practice of how to utilize the correct technique in each situation, chances are slim that you will have much success in taekwondo competition sparring. This choreography, this harmonizing or giving over to the body will allow it to perform without the constraints of the subjective mind, which will shut down and become aware. *In the end, it is this awareness, and who has the most of it, that will determine who will win the fight.*

4. The development of strategies that will maximize my abilities and minimize my shortcomings. For instance, when I was a Second Degree Black Belt I had an unstoppable right side kick. Each person is different physically, emotionally and mentally. Each of us has certain talents and weaknesses. Training for competition sparring brings out both our strengths and weaknesses. In order to excel in martial art you must learn how to constantly struggle with your weaknesses. For instance, when I was a Second Degree Black Belt I had an unstoppable right side kick. Then I blew out my left knee. I could no longer plant with my left leg. As I rehabilitated, I began to work on my balance, strength and stability with my right leg. As my left leg began to heal I practiced side kicking with my left leg. When I was well enough to go back into the ring I had developed a powerful left side kick. It was no longer a weakness but a great strength to be able to fight on both sides with equal capacity. Now I could change stances to match my strength to any situation. Always struggling with your weaknesses will create in

you a certain *capacity for doing.* This is a powerful force that you can take with you into any situation. This capacity for doing will eventually weld all of the different parts of yourself into a *single, harmonious and willful human being.* Ponder upon this. This is your strategy and your goal.

Do not forget your strengths. Remember, most fighters come at you with their strengths. Try to make your strengths *unbeatable.* Do not become complacent, arrogant or dejected when you meet someone who is better than you. If you do, you will lose heart and your-self-love will become wounded. You will want to quit. For example, take a taekwondo student who is superior because of natural talent. Suppose he or she is gifted with extraordinary physical abilities and needs to practice very little. Techniques come easy for them because they do not have to develop their body. They rise naturally to the head of the class. They produce great forms and win in sparring almost all the time. Their ego is inflated because they are the "class darling" and the instructor constantly coos over them.

However over a period of time, those with less fortunate physical stature who dedicate themselves to training, struggle with their weaknesses and persevere through all kinds of adversity, gradually catch up with the one who has natural talent but does not exert themselves beyond what has been given to them. Then the day comes, because of their efforts, those who have committed to a real striving, subdue the natural talent. Then the talented one becomes distraught, does not get the glory they are used getting so easily and do not know how to handle the situation in which they are not the best. At this time they seem to lose interest and drop out of class. The others, who see the great value of their efforts, go on to be Masters or World Champions.

My Strategy

When I was about fourteen, I had two friends that were interested in martial art. At that time in the 1960's, we idolized Chuck Norris, Bruce Lee, Bill Wallace, Mike Stone and Ed Parker. Back then there was very little organized martial art and we basically learned from books. I still have the book by Masutatsu Omatsu called, *This is Karate.* We practiced in our garages, with heavy bags, balls and all kinds of pads. One of my friends,

Jack Hebert, had the perfect body for martial art. He was about five feet ten inches, thickly muscled and had lighting reflexes. Jack became our leader and ate and slept martial art. He developed all kinds of training methods and was the first to video tape his techniques. I still have those videos and train with them. He was always trying to find out *what really works*. In order to put our skills to that test, we began to wander the streets at night in search of challenges. We got in fights all the time and did all kinds of daredevil stunts. We would walk fence lines to develop balance, climb anything and everything from church steeples to the three story public library in town, all at night. We would jump from roof tops to develop our tumbling skills, pounded macawara boards to toughen our fists and leaped over saw horses to increase our jumping ability. We wore black at night and practiced hiding and sneaking up on people like ninjas. Among many of Jack's incredible skills was his leaping ability. I saw him leap straight up and front kick the light bulb out in the eight foot ceiling of his garage, do a flip and land on his feet! His specialty was a running jump side kick. He could break a two by four, six feet high with this technique. His reverse hook kick was awesome. Once we went to an informal gathering of martial artists to demonstrate our skills. There was a medicine ball suspended on a rope from the ceiling. People were showing their power by punching and kicking it. Jack did a jump reverse hook kick on it with such force that it broke the rope and sent the ten pound medicine ball flying into the audience. It hit a man full in the chest and knocked him out of his chair! Jack's side kick was so powerful and so fast that you could not get near him sparring or you paid for it. Jack taught me the side kick and made me practice it until I could not walk.

When I returned to martial art (taekwondo) in my late forties, I realized that I still had a wicked side kick. Therefore, my sparring strategy was born.

1. Everything comes off of the defensive side kick. *I know what I am going to do*. No matter what the opponent does, I side kick.

2. Stop whatever the opponent is trying to do by side kicking. When someone attacks you they have a thought of what they want to do. If you can interfere or stop this plan, it disrupts their thought process and stops their initiative. Most people only have one favorite technique

because they have been successful with it. It is their strength and they come at you with it. If you can stop it then the momentum of the fight shifts in your favor. Your opponent has to reevaluate before they can continue. In the meantime your choreography training takes over and you score. *This is when the real sparring begins.*

3. Stop their technique before it starts. Treat a step toward you like a kick. When they step toward you, side kick to the belt. This is called *Stop Hit.* Wherever the belt goes, so goes the person. The point one or two inches above the belt is *where a person's will is expressed.* It is also a very vulnerable spot to hurt someone, not only physically but psychologically.

4. Make them beat your side kick. I used to call it the "the battle of the big dogs" because when strange dogs meet, they try to look bigger than they are. They usually do not fight unless they are evenly matched and neither will back down. A similar thing happens when you meet an opponent that has as good a side kick as you do. Every fight I would make my opponent try to beat my side kick. This led to some great battles and bruised legs. The big dog would force the other fighter to fight another way. The important thing to understand is that a really good side kick takes away a frontal assault and usually, the strength of the opponent. *It forces them to fight your fight.*

5. When you stop or interfere with the *intent* of your opponent it creates a momentary opening that can be exploited by your sparring choreography. *Practice your choreography.*

My Choreography Training

Defense

1. Number one side kick, reverse side kick or jump reverse side kick

2. Number one side kick, punch, punch, number two round kick, jump front kick

3. Number one side kick, reverse heel kick or reverse hook kick

4. Number one side kick, hook kick, round kick

5. Number one repeat side kick

6. Number one side kick, jump side kick

7. V-out, block, number one side kick (both sides)

8. V-out, block, and number two jump round kick (both sides)

9. V-out, block, hook punch (both sides)

10. V-out reverse heel kick (both sides)

Offense

1. Skipping side kick, punch-punch, reverse side kick, hook kick, heel kick or jump reverse side kick

2. Skipping round kick, punch-punch, reverse side, hook or heel kick or jump reverse side kick

3. Skipping hook kick, punch-punch, reverse side, hook or heel kick or jump reverse side kick

4. Step, jump side kick, punch-punch reverse heel kick

5. Step, step reverse side kick with opposite leg

6. V-out and repeat 1, 2, 3 (V-out both sides)

I know this is repeating the same techniques that are listed in sparring chapter, but it is worth it to emphasize to you the importance of choreography.

Chapter 11

*The only thing of any
real and lasting intrinsic value,
lies in the
Objectivity
of the moment.*

The Sparring Mind (Simultaneity)

As the title of this book suggests, the inner aspect of martial art is the core of this work. We all see the outer aspect, that is the development of the physical body, but few of us understand the great aphorism, *for every outer manifestation there must also be a corresponding inner one.* The inner aspect of human experience cannot be accessed by any sense organ, yet without its presence there can be no outward expression through the body. But even deeper than that, the growth of the *inner life of man* can be manifested beyond the physical body. For me, martial art's great value has been the development of my inner life. In the mind, the inner aspect is the accessibility of a different state of consciousness.

The "consciousness" we are all enveloped in is called subjective consciousness. What is subjectivity? It is the relative experiencing of the five senses as interpreted by the hardwiring of the mind. This state of consciousness is always changing and repeating, only perceiving reality in a small, finite way. It is like going into a dark house with a candle. The light of consciousness probes here and there, constantly bouncing around, revealing small bits of this and that in the room, but never seeing the entire contents of the room and how they are related. It is with this apparatus of the mind that we think we know our world and ourselves. We never even suspect that there are other rooms in our house. Every day, this subjective mind constantly repeats the same functions - associating, identifying, going over our inventory, anticipating and remembering. Every day, beginning as you awaken, this subjective mind is constantly going over the same thought process of pigeonholing information, retrieving it according to external impressions and reacting to it. Every day, it constantly goes over its inventory of thoughts and obsesses about the "burning question of the day." It is always in constant motion. This is the only mind we know. It has been called the *formatory apparatus.*

The force of life driving the functions of the subjective mind has long been known by ancient esoteric groups, and I have been fortunate enough to be involved with two such groups. I wanted to reveal these functions so that you can begin to observe your own thoughts and how they relate to the sparring mind.

Mechanical Aspects of the Mind (Group I)

1. Circling thoughts

2. Associations

3. Inner conversations or inner dialogue

4. Imaginings

5. Constant inventorying

6. Identification

7. Constant comparison or dichotomy of thought

Conscious Potential of the Mind

1. The Watchman

2. The Director

3. The Awakener

Mechanical Aspects of the Mind (Group II)

1. Imagination

2. Identification

3. Plurality

4. Inner accounting

5. Internal considering

6. Lying

7. Self-justification

8. Pretending

9. False pictures of one's self

10. Negative attitudes

11. Acquired opinions

12. Mechanical reactions

13. Vanity, pride, self-complacency and self-love

14. Anticipation and remembering

15. Smugness

Conscious Potential of the Mind

1. Observation

2. Impartiality

3. Simultaneity (being now)

4. Awareness

If you have never questioned the functions of your mind, then you have never considered its limitations and the potentiality for its growth into other areas. You have accepted the mechanical aspects of your mind as the totality of its function and are totally immersed in a cage of endless repetition. When confronted with the reality of sparring, the mechanical aspects of the mind and its very movement are literally of no value and retard your ability to spar on the level needed to win. I am reminded of the movie *The Last Samurai* starring Tom Cruise. When he was practicing with the sword and was confronted with the fact he was too slow, he was told, "Too many minds." Behind this advice is a great truth you need to explore. It is this truth that is the basis of this chapter.

The Rhythm of the Subjective Process

The next thing you need to understand is that the subjective mind has a certain rhythm, or period, or vibration rate. This rhythm is the rate at which the thought process arises, manifests and subsides. In general, it takes about three seconds to receive external perceptions, form a conception of these perceptions and initiate a bodily response. The explanation of this process is that the perception is taken in through the eye to the fovea centralis, then to the optic nerve where it is transmitted to the cerebral cortex. Here it is mixed with former impressions (memory) to create a gestalt (an organized whole that is perceived as more than the sum of its parts). This gestalt is routed to the appropriate center of the cerebellum. Here begins the afferent stimulation of the musculature involved with the physical response. Then the body reacts. If you express this "thought period" as rhythm count, it would be a one or two count. This is the average time most people can take in impressions, formulate a thought and then react consciously to a situation. Even people with "gifted" minds, who we call geniuses, cannot get past a four count. Sparring takes place at an eight count, or even a sixteenth count.

I am going to digress here for a moment to prevent a misunderstanding of what I just said. Do not mistake this process with "mechanical thought." Mechanical thought is observed when people carry on conversations that seem to be lighting fast, faster than the above process. This type of thought, the lowest form of thought, is what we all partake in under the guise of "communication." In actuality, it is simply the "associative process" reacting to preconditioned words and phrases that have been cubby-holed in one's memory and released instantaneously to the external perception of someone else's preconditioned words and phrases. In reality, the only thing transmitted is superficial words and phrases where the meaning is assumed by the speaker to be understood by the listener. The word superficial is used because both the speaker and the listener assume that each has the exact same understanding of the words used. However, all words are based on experience and unless both participants have had the exact same experience, neither will understand what the other really means. However, both will assume they do. Let us take for example the word "man." If you ask a doctor what a man is he will say that he is a biological organism with bones, muscles, organs of circulation and a nervous system, etc. If you ask a priest what a man is he will say a man is a being made in the image of God with a Soul. If you ask a woman what a man is she will say he is a male. The meaning of a word depends on one's experience and frame of reference. Think about this when you are engaged in conversation with someone else. What really passes between you, what have each of you really understood from the conversation?

In returning to the rhythm of the intellect, you can see by the speed necessary to spar, an eight count or a sixteen count, that the ordinary mind simply cannot keep up with the activity of the body, which operates at a much higher speed than the mind. It is 30,000 times faster to be more accurate. Yet the mind, due to its preconditioned state, still tries to control the body under sparring conditions. This is something you need to understand. *You need to shut down the mind, as you know it, to free the body of its influence.* In Zen they call this *No Mind.* In western sports they call this *The Zone.* In esoteric circles they call this *Simultaneity,* or simply *Freedom.* In some forms of yoga, this is accomplished by increasingly complicated mental exercises and meditation. In monastic settings it is accomplished by constant prayer, chanting and musical rhythms (like the Whirling Dervishes). In martial art, this is accomplished by elevating the period of body vibrations. The simplest form of raising the vibratory state of the body is by *bouncing or hopping.* Yes, simply hopping while sparring will shut down the associative process of the mind. What is left is simply *awareness.*

This awareness is an entirely different state of consciousness. It is *now.* Being now fundamentally changes the perceptual process by bypassing the frontal cortex and mid brain. It also changes how visual perception is routed to the cerebellum. Instead of the "sight picture" being routed to the fovea centralis and frontal cortex, the vision "expands," so to speak, to take in the *entirety or totality of the visual experience.* The development of the total visual experience is the result of the development of the *peripheral vision.* The peripheral vison can instantaneously detect movement, the speed of the movement, the direction of the movement and the *intent of the movement.* Stimuli from the peripheral vison goes directly to the cerebellum, which can then give an instantaneous response by the body, *provided the body's responses have been adequately trained to produce the precise, correct physical response.* This awareness is an entirely different *level of being.* It is this level of being you need to cultivate in yourself in order to spar with excellence. By the way, people who live very close to Mother Nature naturally develop this awareness. This level of awareness is called *seeing* in esoteric circles. For me, this is the inner reason for sparring, to develop this type of awareness.

Flicker Fusion

There is another physiological process that limits the ability of a person to react. It is called *flicker fusion*. When light enters the eye in the form of a visual impression, a chemical reaction takes place on the retina, converting the impression to afferent nerve firings that travel to the brain for interpretation. The ability of the retina to convert impressions into a nervous flow of firings is limited in the human being to about fifty or sixty firings per second. In other words, a series of pictures are sent to the brain fifty or sixty times per second. Most movement we experience with the eye seems to be a smooth motion picture of the event taking place, without spaces or gaps. In reality however, these seemingly smooth movements are actually still pictures with gaps in between them. The brain knits them together to make them appear as a seamless event. Just like cartoons, movies and television, we see these without interruption because the still pictures are moving faster than the eye's flicker fusion rate. If we take an old movie that was hand cranked, the gaps between the still pictures can be seen, because the speed is below our flicker fusion rate. This is how the eye, in reality, sees things. Our fluorescent lights operate at sixty cycles per second. We do not notice that they flicker unless the bulb begins to go out and the cycles go below sixty per second, then we see the flickering. The flicker fusion rate is determined by the falling of the light on our fovea centralis, which is packed with cones for rich color recognitions. The peripheral vision of our eye is mostly rods, which only see shades of gray. The signals of fovea centralis are programed through the long route of the frontal lobe and formatory apparatus, then through the mid brain and finally through the cerebellum. Signals of the peripheral vision bypass this route and go directly to the cerebellum.

On an interesting note, dogs and probably many other animals, see very little color but more shades of yellow, blue and gray. They have flicker fusion rates of seventy to eighty times per second. This explains how they can catch balls and other objects or animals at speeds that defy our eye. It also explains how they seem to know what we are going to do before we even do it. They are always watching us and perceive our direction and intent of motion as if they were psychic. They must see us as if we were an old movie, frame after frame with intervals in between.

Therefore, if we bounce or hop while sparring our body can reach an eighth or a sixteenth count and we can achieve a shutting down of the associative process. The result is that our visual perception of motion goes d-i-r-e-c-t-l-y to our cerebellum. This is when things seem to s-l-o-w d-o-w-n or become like slow motion. In addition, we begin to see things in flicker fusion slices, or single photographs of your opponent's actions. Another phenomenon also takes place that is rare and beautiful, in my opinion. That is, you and your opponent become *objective*. In other words, you are out of your body, watching *the body* punch, kick and move. There is a sense of yourself existing and observing, without being attached to the body. This is simultaneity, this is the zone, this is no mind and this is freedom.

If you could diagram the difference it would look like this:

Subjectivity: perception – thought process – reaction - response

Objectivity: perception – awareness - response

If you were truly in this state of objectivity, then after the fight, when you "come down" from the fight, there would be no detailed memory of what took place. This is because the subjective mind, being shut down during the fight, can have no subjective memory of the event. I would always try to get someone to video each fight of mine, so I could review it later. In some of the fights, I saw that my body was bouncing so fast that it was literally vibrating. I was now, I was in the zone, and I could remember nothing when I came down. Like any endeavor, it takes practice and time to learn how to access this state and stay in it and move around in it. It is a state with a higher vibration rate. It is difficult even to know what this state is, because you are used to the gross subjective state with its gross energies and lower vibration rate. Objectivity is so different. It has a different "taste," if you will. Here I am reminded again of Miyomato Mushasi's words.

"The more and more you seek the spirit of a thing, the more and more the Spirit of the Thing will reveal itself to you."

Flicker Fusion and Plyometric Training

We have learned that we can allow visual pictures to be transmitted to the body almost instantly with peripheral vision by shutting down the fore and mid brain and executing a response through the body. This is one aspect of training that has to be developed. However, the execution of the bodily response also has to be trained, so that the entire process of the technique can be utilized instantly. The recruitment, training and execution of the fast twitch muscle fibers involved in the technique is equally important, so that a seamless cycle of sight picture to technique can be achieved. Plyometric training, as we spoke of in previous chapters, is the catalyst that brings all the different aspects into harmony. What good is it to shut down the mind if the technique cannot be executed in the same instant? By practicing plyometric training, the *entire muscle can be activated from a single sight picture.* If you can bounce or hop four times a second, then any given sight picture of the flicker fusion can be responded to four times faster. For me, a type of *synchronicity* is formed inside one's self that raises your level of being in sparring and opens you up to a new world.

Identification

As soon as you came into this world and your five senses began to function, you began to attach yourself to the world. Instinct took over for many things - breathing, swallowing, drinking and crawling, etc. As your mind began to function, you started to put attention on things. For every skilled act the body has learned, a small amount of mental attention was attached while learning it. Even now as an adult, every non-instinctual posture and motion that has been learned still has a piece of attention attached to it and it functions when the movement is made. This is why your postures, gestures, facial expressions, tone of voice and movements have definite thoughts, feelings, attitudes and "I's" associated with their expressions. Every skill you have ever learned, at first began with a mental attachment. Then, by trial and error, over time you converted the thought process into a physical dexterity. Therefore, if you could observe every learned physical activity, you could notice that a small piece of attention, a remnant belonging to the early efforts, converted the thought of the activity into action. This is called identification. The mind is identified with every physical activity. Every seemingly unconscious or mechanical movement, like walking, still has a small piece or remnant of your attention attached to it.

In learning martial art, the exact same process occurs. When you first learned a high block, the instructor described it to you, demonstrated it for you and then asked you to do it. You put mental attention onto the process of learning the block and gradually transformed the attention to physical movement. Then you practiced it over and over again, until the thought process decreased and the mechanical memory of the body took over and you could perform the movement automatically. The movement now became a bodily memory, and the mental attention needed to actuate it decreased. However, even now, when you can mechanically perform the high block, a small amount of the mind is still associated with that move. A small amount of mental attention remains attached to the high block. This identification of the mind with physical technique slows down the technique or gives it away to your opponent. This is called "telegraphing." You cannot have this identification in sparring, it will slow your techniques down. As soon as you wait to see the effect of the technique you just threw, then you are identified with the technique.

Looking back to when I began to spar as a colored belt, this mental aspect resulted in a tenseness or tightness of my whole body. All my movements were jerky without control. One of my instructors, Master Randy Carvin was the best sparrer in our school. While sparring me one day he noticed this tenseness and showed me how to relax while sparring. This one episode changed my whole journey in taekwondo and my ability to fight. Thank you Sir!

The Ten Thousand Rule

The only way to squeeze out this identification of the mind is to do the technique consciously thousands of times to truly make the movement an automatic reflex. This is also called, *giving over to the body that which belongs to it*. The Ten Thousand Rule is the only way to do this. You must do the technique ten thousand times, willfully, within a certain period of time, to make the memory of the body take over this task and relieve the mind of this burden. If you watch a child learn things, say to throw or catch a ball, then you will notice they will do it thousands of times before it becomes automatic. All of our mechanical bodily movements were learned like this. Once this is done, the tiny amount of attention that was bound up in the technique is released and returns to the mind in the form of awareness. *This is important, this is what you need to do with each technique you use in sparring*. Going back to the chapter on acceleration and practicing your techniques in this way will gradually free the body from intellectual hindrance and turn the technique over to the peripheral sight picture. Always begin from your fighting stance, with knees bent, in ready relaxation with your hands in proper guard while accentuating a proper chamber. Then after perfect extension, immediately rechamber with balance and retain the rechamber for an instant, ready for another kick, before returning your leg to the floor. Gather yourself again in your fighting stance, knees bent, and repeat. *Remember, you will fight like you train.* Practice diligently, always focused on your aim to win.

For years I had one workout per week devoted solely to acceleration techniques on the bag. Start with the basic four techniques - side kick, round kick, hook kick and reverse side kick. Add others when these have been mastered.

Choreography

Just like form practice, you must also practice your sparring combinations. In the ring, anything can happen, but in reality, *certain things happen over and over again*! Think of your acceleration drills as the tip of a spear, and the shaft of the spear are the movements that get you into position to strike.

Divide the choreography of your moves into offensive and defensive. Begin all your sparring combinations from bouncing (remember plyometrics). Always strive to be bilateral, doing your combinations from both right and left sparring stances. This serves a three-fold purpose. First, remember the aphorism, *always strive to struggle with your weaknesses and maintain your strengths.* Less-experienced fighters will always spar from one side or the other and are inflexible to the constantly changing situations of a fight. It is similar to fixed fortifications in the battle of armies - they are monuments to stupidity. For an opposing mobile army will always outflank them. You must always strive for excellence with all of your combinations from both sides so you can take advantage of any opening and not reveal to your opponent any weakness on one side or the other. Second, choreographing your moves from both sides allows you to probe the weaknesses of your opponent in either an open or closed stance. Third, your bilateral ability will reduce your reaction time and take advantage of the target opening up under any condition. Your mobility is an incredible asset in sparring (remember the four point drill in the plyometric chapter). I would practice my choreography after practicing the acceleration drills. Here are the choreography drills I would practice.

Offense:

1. Skipping side kick, punch-punch, reverse side kick, hook or heel kick or jump reverse side kick.

2. Skipping round kick, punch-punch, reverse side kick, hook or heel kick or jump reverse side kick.

3. Skipping hook kick, punch-punch, reverse side kick, hook or heel kick or jump reverse side kick.

4. Step-step jump side kick, punch-punch reverse heel kick.

5. Step-step reverse side kick.

6. V-out and repeat 1, 2, 3 (V-out both sides).

These are highly aggressive offensive moves with commitment to engage, score or to run your opponent out of bounds. Even if you are a defensive fighter, at some point you may get behind and have to go on offense to catch up. If I lost a point and was behind, *I would try to make it up immediately!*

Defense:

1. Jump back, side kick, punch-punch, reverse heel kick.

2. Jump back, punch-punch, side kick, reverse heel kick.

3. Jump back, side kick, reverse side kick or jump reverse side kick.

4. V-out, side kick, punch-punch (V-out both sides), number two round kick.

5. V-out, jump round kick, punch-punch (V-out both sides).

6. Step back while changing stance, side kick, and punch-punch.

7. Step back while changing stance, number two round kick (or jump round) punch-punch.

8. Lean back, outer forearm block, hook punch.

All defensive choreography should be done from bouncing and should be practiced on both sides. Remember, choreographed moves are a lead into battle. After their completion, you should make the jump into awareness, and the body should take over without conscious effort. Then the real sparring begins.

Every Technique Has a Counter

Just as crucial as choreography is the knowledge of every technique you will encounter. You must learn the strength and weakness of every technique. In defensive fighting, you must avoid, block or stop the strength of the offensive technique. The counter technique comes when the weakness of the offensive technique opens up. Generally, your knowledge of each offensive technique will allow you to position yourself to take advantage of its weakness. Again, you must practice these counter techniques until there is no thought process. Once this is achieved by the Ten Thousand rule, you can actually "see" the weakness coming and respond to it not too much or too little, but exactly what is required.

Offensive kicking techniques are most vulnerable in two places. The first is when the opponent is stepping toward you to close the gap, right before the chamber. This is when you must employ the *Stop Hit*. The stop hit is Bruce Lee's term for stopping your opponent before his technique gets started. In his book, *Tao of Jeet Kune Do - The Way of the Intercepting Fist*, he details these techniques. The most effective stop hit technique is the number one side kick, or reverse or jump reverse side kick. If you can stop your opponent's offensive technique, it will disrupt his rhythm, upset his timing and create doubt as to what to do. This usually causes a reaction to try the technique again, which you will either be waiting for, or you will have already gone over to the offense when you see his hesitation. To be effective at a stop hit with a side kick, you must practice it until it is the fastest, most powerful and most deadly technique in your arsenal. It becomes the *leading edge of your will*. At the 1999 World Championships, in my first Top Ten competition, I was injured and could only do a side kick on one side, but what a side kick it was! I won my first World Title with a number side kick and punches. After that, I realized the tremendous advantage you have if you have a great side kick. It changes the entire fight and forces your opponent to alter his strategy to get around your side kick. You control the fight. From then on, I made every opponent try to beat my side kick. It is called "Big Dog," when the first move of every fight is to find out who had the best side kick. If my opponent was hugely bigger than me or had the best side kick, then I would employ the V-out footwork to avoid his side kick and position myself for a reactive counter side kick, round kick or punch. This strategy has served me well!

Know Your Opponent

I would try to get someone to video my fights, usually my wife, my instructor, a spectator or even an opponent. This was invaluable to me. It showed my weaknesses and strengths, as well as those of my opponents. It also revealed to me my opponent's strategy and way of fighting that they were perhaps unconscious of. It exposed their reactions to each technique and openings they did not prepare for. Videoing your form is also invaluable to get an objective view of your execution and to compare the "sense" of your technique to actually see how it is perceived by others. I can't overemphasize the importance of having an objective view of your performance. Other than your instructor's comments on your form and fighting, a video of your actions is the only real truth available to your subjective mind.

Once you can pair your sense of the technique with the objective view of your body, the body memory will never forget, and you will strive for that "sense of the technique" every time you perform.

Developing Conscience

The conscience is the maturing force of the feeling center. The mechanical connections between the body and the feeling center formed long ago in childhood. We have no control over our mechanical feelings. In other words, every feeling is expressed immediately through the body. If someone calls you a fool, your body tenses, you become angry and want to hit them, while the corresponding feeling of outrage of being treated so badly floods your solar plexus. If someone says you are a "good little boy," your body relaxes as that warm, fuzzy feeling strokes your vanity and expands over the whole of you. Your body is literally a playground for your feelings. Your day is nothing but a carousel of mechanical feelings reacting to life situations that impinge upon you. Mechanical feelings are the lowest expression of the feeling center. Your main mechanical feelings are likes and dislikes, self-justification, self-love, self-absorption, vanity, pride and the lowest of the low - negative emotions.

To be able to make the body train to achieve the goal set by your mind requires the development of a new aspect of the feeling center that is usually undeveloped in people. It is called conscience. Conscience is not the nebulous conception of right and wrong. Nor is it the idea of an angel sitting on your right shoulder and the devil sitting on your left shoulder in a constant battle for control. Nor is it morality that is conscience. Morality is culturally different. What is moral in one country or culture is immoral in another. Morality is also different from one family teaching to the next and one religion to the next. Real conscience can only be developed by the introduction of a serious aim or purpose in your life. It is an inner aspect that is conscious in origin and must be remembered over and over again when one has given an essence oath to oneself to achieve a long and difficult goal.

Suppose I have the aim to be World Champion. I have sat in front of the mirror for a long time and asked myself, "Who am I, what am I. What do I wish for my life?" After long consideration and pondering, I have made an essence oath to myself. "I-wish-to-be-World-Champion." This is the first force, the active force.

After you have decided on your goal, then the law-conformable obstacles immediately become visible to you and form to retard your efforts. These are the retarding forces of your striving. It is not that they were not there the whole time, but you have never had such an aim before, therefore you never realized their existence. The body is lazy and overweight, the work is hard, there is not enough time and your training cuts into your family time. You are not fast enough, your techniques are not good enough and your flexibility stinks. Soreness prevents you from training as often as you need to. You become injured and can't train for a long time. No one around you shares your aim, no one else cares. You have no place to train by yourself. This is the second force - the negative force. You have underestimated your opponent by your own mechanical way of being.

This is when you must begin to develop the third force, the reconciling force. This reconciling force is your Wish. It is your emotional wish to become World Champion. It is the realization that the vision of the mind cannot "make" the body do it. The connections are not there. It requires a tremendous motivating force, an emotional wish to constantly pull the body in the direction of your aim. This *Wish* is different than a mechanical want or desire, which are cheap. Desires and wants constantly arise and clamor to be satisfied and you succumb, day in and day out. A Wish is a conscious motivating force that wakes you up every day and reminds you of the aim you have set for yourself. It has to be on the same level as a drowning man seeking air. The wish has to have that force. A wish, manifested daily, over a long period of time, grows and develops into a conscience. Every day it questions you, reminds you of the oath you took, of your aim. It comes into every aspect of your life and manifests itself as a question to your conscience.

"Is this what I do now, in conformity with my aim, or is it not?"

This question is the food for the growth of your conscience. If you go back on your word, if you continue to ignore the fact that what you are doing or not doing is against your aim, then you must admit that you are lying to yourself.

I promise you, if you develop a conscience, you can achieve anything!

Chapter 12

The more and more you seek
the spirit of the thing,
the more and more the Spirit of the Thing
will reveal Itself to you.

Miyamoto Musashi
The Book of Five Rings

*A higher level of being
is an approach
toward unity in
one's self.*

The Value of Forms

A form, Poomsae or Kata is practiced in almost every martial art. It is the stringing together of a series of techniques into a continuous movement of various lengths. In many styles, the form is so arranged that it is like fighting an imaginary opponent. It is not unlike a dance routine, except the techniques are stances, blocks, strikes and kicks, and there is usually no music choreographed to it.

Where did form come from, why is it a part of almost all martial art and why is practicing it so important?

Originally, martial art form had a spiritual beginning. By spiritual, I mean it had knowledge that cannot be accessed by the intellect. These forms appeared in the world because of the practice of monks in monasteries in the Middle East, India, Tibet and China. I know this because I was fortunate enough to participate for many years in "Sacred Dances" that were passed down unchanged, from generation to generation, for thousands of years in esoteric schools that perhaps originated in Sumerian times. They were very difficult. In each dance, each body part was performing a different posture or movement simultaneously. Each dance was choreographed to special music, specifically to that dance. Many dances also included a mental activity, something like a mantra. There were three levels – beginner, intermediate and advanced. The originators of these dances, or "movements" as we called them, understood the needs of the human body and the laws that govern it. In addition, they used these movements as a vestibule or vessel of objective knowledge to be transmitted to future generations for the benefit and growth of their being. They understood that certain knowledge, inner knowledge, could be transmitted exactly without being changed by the intellect, through time to those yet unborn. Then those recipients, whose being would have reached the level to receive this form, could "decipher" this knowledge and use it for their growth and development as a real human being. This is called *objective* art. Other forms or remnants of objective art can be found on earth in music and architecture. This type of art is also found in script, in the form of legends, parables and myths. For instance, one esoteric group had devised a certain postural alphabet. A person who learned this alphabet, could perform these dances and "read" the knowledge embedded in them. One movement I was privileged to watch was the orchestration of The Law of Three and the Law of Octaves. It was an amazing demonstration. However, all doctrines, art and knowledge, spiritual or otherwise, deteriorate with time into dogma (mechanical practice of the outward form without the inner meaning), if it is not transformed again by a special person. Why does this happen?

Take any great teacher from history, spiritual or otherwise, who has founded a teaching that attracts people to them. Their level of being is so elevated that it attracts those who have a corresponding need to develop this being in themselves. As a result, a group of disciples form around this great teacher to emulate him by taking his instructions. These disciples, after years of following this teaching, develop their being according to their understanding, personality and efforts. However, none of the disciples are able to absorb the teaching in its entirety. None can master the Master. As a result, after the passing of this great Master, each disciple becomes a teacher. Yet over time, the entirety of the original teaching is modified through this disciple's personality, predisposition and the crystallization of their own efforts, or level of being. After the Master dies, none of the disciples can fully take his place. If another does take his place, the original teaching has already become modified to some extent, and the level of being begins to deteriorate. Perhaps this new teacher is interested in one aspect of the teaching at the expense of another. Maybe this new teacher has more ability in one area than another, thereby shifting the entire teaching in that direction. If there are several disciples of more or less equal being, the teaching is fragmented into an equivalent number of pieces, with each disciple expounding it in a slightly different way. When these disciples have their own students, they teach whatever they are capable, which causes the original teaching to fragment further and the level of being is reduced even more. In addition to the diluted lineage of such fragmentation, the introduction into the world of this original teaching begins to mix with the influences of the ordinary world. It is sad that sometimes, these fragmented lineages actually compete with one another as the "true way."

Therefore at some point, the original teaching becomes lost and the doctrine is replaced by dogma. People still repeat the outward form mechanically, but the essence of the teaching, the real reason for its existence, the real benefit for mankind, has been lost.

If we take the original, pure teaching and label it an ES influence, or esoteric, then we can say that the fragmentation process changes the pure teaching into a mixed teaching which we will call an M influence. The M influence, still near the original source, spreads the teaching into world influences, which we will call EX influences, or exoteric. So if you or I are far-removed from the ES influence of the Master, we are basically receiving M influences mixed with the ordinary EX influences of the world. So it is with martial art teachings. *The study of influences is important in order to understand what forces we obey.*

Does this mean that martial art today is not worthy of participation? Not at all. However, because the level of the world practitioners, the essence or *inner aspect* of the art has been forgotten and dogma is the norm. There is much misinformation and dis-information. I say this not in a negative way, but as a fact. One of the great aphorisms says, *for every outer manifestation, there must always be a corresponding inner one.* EX influences or world influences, project the outside manifestation to the practitioner. You must find the inner, the esoteric or ES influences on your own.

Miyamoto Musashi, Japan's greatest swordsman, put it this way.

"The more and more you seek the spirit of the thing, the more and more the Spirit of the Thing will reveal Itself to you."

So let us find out what the spirit of form is, why it is important for your growth as a human being and why you should practice it often and make it part of your life.

Form as a Receptacle of Objective Art

Art is part of our lives. It surrounds us. It is within us. It is a unique aspect of human expression. It seems to arise from a deep need to express one's self to the world. The art we are most familiar with are the visual arts like painting, drawing and sculpture. Writing is an art form. Music is an art form. Dance is an art form. Architecture is an art form. Martial art is an art form. It is only the medium of the manifestation that makes it unique.

However, art today is different from ancient art. Today's art could be called subjective art, because the emphasis comes from the horizontal or EX influences of the world at large. Subjective art is what people create spontaneously, as it were, from their own life experiences and desires. Many different classes or types of art have arisen in the course of history, and people are attracted to one class or type according to their predisposition, exposure and experience. So it is with martial art.

Ancient art, however, is different than contemporary art. Ancient art is an embodiment of knowledge that cannot be accessed by the intellect as we know it. Ancient art, because of its inaccessibility by the intellect, cannot be altered or mutated by the thought process. This kind of art is called objective art. An objective piece of art was created consciously to contain knowledge that the creator wished to transmit to generations yet unborn. It is a definite mathematical expression that can be transmitted from generation to generation without being changed. The uniqueness of objective art is that it is only accessible by people who have developed their level of being up to the threshold where the knowledge in the art form is accessible or can be understood. It could be called *being art*. Many examples of objective art still remain on earth today. The ones that come to mind from my experience are the pyramids, the sphinx and certain ancient temples and cathedrals. These are objective architectural forms. There are objective books like the Bible, the Mahabharata, the Quran, and the Upanishads. In my opinion, The Book of Five Rings is an example of objectivity in martial art. Dance is another area where examples of objective art are expressed. I have participated in Sacred Dances that were developed in remote temples, centuries ago. These were transmitted unchanged from generation to generation to the present. It taught me that the expression of the physical body can be used as an objective art form.

When we were young, my wife and I traveled to Egypt. We went to the Egyptian Museum in Cairo. While browsing through the museum, we came upon a huge sculpture of an Egyptian Priestess in a kneeling posture with her left arm thrust out to the side and her palm down. Her right arm was bent with her palm placed over her heart. Her head was lowered as if in prayer. My wife and I looked at each other wide-eyed in amazement and my body shook involuntarily. *This was the exact same posture found in one of the obligatory movements that we practiced!* We understood then, the tremendous significance of objective art, and the effect it could have on one's inner life.

Now we come to martial art. Could it be that a martial art form was a vessel of objective knowledge, inserted purposefully by those who understood and to be experienced by today's practitioner? Is there more to martial art form than the external manifestation? Is there a deeper meaning, an inner aspect that makes the practice of form worthwhile to develop one's level of being? What is the real reason to practice form? Is it objective art?

From my experience, there are three aspects to form. The outer aspect, the inner aspect and the residual aspect.

The outer aspect of form practice is well-defined in most systems. The best I have experienced are the Ten Attributes described by the American Taekwondo Association. Normally, these attributes are not fully developed in Western Culture. Although not specifically the result of the practice of form, the attributes seem to be inherently developed by form practice. The reason for the development of these attributes is because the inner aspect of form practice contributes to the growth of one's inner life. The attributes are likened to the fruit of the plant, which is produced by the functioning of the roots, trunk, branches and leaves. Each form produces its own type of fruit.

The inner aspect is the functioning of the level of being of the individual. It cannot be accessed by the five senses, but when it leaves, we say that there is no life. It is spirit.

The residual aspect of form practice is the gradual overflow of the development of attributes into all areas of life, beyond the actual practice. It is like a vessel that overflows from the container that surrounds it. It is the change in the level of one's being. It is the growth of one's essential essence. It is becoming what one really is.

The Inner Aspect

In order for you to understand the value of forms, you must try to understand three things. You are not one entity. You are made up of three independent centers, or totalities of functions or brains. It has been said that the centers are jelly-like in nature and life experiences are impressed upon them. This causes the centers to congeal or crystalize over time into rigid, mechanical actors that continuously repeat the same expressions. These centers are not unified, nor are they composed of the same materials. You are existing as many and not one. Each brain is oblivious to the existence of the other two. Take any time during the day. Suppose you are going to work. Your mind is anticipating the upcoming day. Perhaps you are upset because another driver cut you off, and your body is tense from the adrenalin of the near wreck. You are so identified that you do not know that your body exists. Your feelings are reflecting the thumping heart and the swelling anxiety in your solar plexus. Your body is non-existent because of your identification with the swarming thoughts about your episode. Each center is in its own world. You are not one. This is the typical picture of our being, all the time. The mind is lost in anticipation, recollection, imagination, self-justification, accounting, inner conversations or the dichotomy of mechanical thoughts. Your feelings, left to themselves, use the body as a playground. Excitement, depression, anxiety, anger, desire, aversion, indulgence and attraction pass through the feeling center as randomly as the impressions that come to you each moment. Your body is all about instinct and reacting to external impressions impinging on the sense organs. It is hot, cold, hungry, thirsty, itching, burning, aching, sore, tense, in pain or pleasure and tired all in one day. In addition, the body is pushed around by the flippant feelings that indulge in every thought process. You are not one. You are out of control, yet it is normalcy for you and you constantly say "I." You use the word "I" as if it were nothing, and it is true. You have no permanent *I*.

> *When you do form, your centers are forced to work together.*
> *The mind becomes what it should be, the director. The feeling center*
> *becomes what it should be, the motive force. The body becomes what it*
> *should be, the servant.*

In order for the mind to assume the role as director, first and foremost it must become now. It becomes now from the sense of the body existing. Sensing the body always requires an effort from the mind. This sense may be called the *Sixth Sense*. The sense of the body existing, is observed by the mind in the form of its five physical manifestations. They are posture, movement, gestures, tone of voice and facial expressions. The physical manifestations of the body are always now. The connection between the observing mind and the body forms a special relationship that can be cultivated by form practice. This function of the mind sensing and directing the body is a much higher state of being than ordinary living. It is the beginning of awareness. In ordinary living there is no now, no connection between centers and no awareness of the body existing. This fragmentation of the centers is called *One-Centered Activity.*

In order for the feeling center to grow into a motive force, a special connection must begin between the feelings and the director. This relationship between the mind and the feeling center is formed by the creation of a goal or aim to express the body in a certain way. The constant remembering and striving toward an aim gradually transforms the feeling center into an emotional motive force, or a Wish. The development of a wish is a very high state of being that can animate and control the body. This is called will. Further development of a wish can become a powerful motive force, called conscience. The relationship formed by the function of the director with the conscience of the emotional center is an extremely powerful force and it is a very high level of being. *It is an inner joy. If you can bring a developed conscience into being, you can achieve anything. You can do.*

In order for the body to develop to its fullest potential, it must be controlled by the director and motivated by the conscience. In ordinary life, the body controls the mind and the feelings and it lives in total chaos. The body is constantly driven by desire after desire to be satisfied. Any *directed* thought process is squashed by the body's instinctive drive to satisfy itself. Food, thirst, sex, temperature control, pain and pleasure are endless recurring desires that must be satisfied. The mind and the feelings are too weak to stand against it. But once the body is under control of the director and motivated by the conscience, it can achieve extraordinary feats and accomplish tremendous goals. *This has been called Delight in Movement.*

The most important value of the development of the three centers is the inner aspect - the inner harmony of three becoming one. The esoteric being that is achieved by controlling the body, developing the conscience and transforming the formatory apparatus of the mind into the director is the proper way a human being should be. *He or she should be one.*

The most difficult thing to grasp is participating in the form when the body is free to proceed without interference of the mind. The mind is aware of the body but not attached to it, and the feeling center is free to express itself *without the use of the body.* This is a very, very, very high aim.

This is the real reason for doing form - to grow up as a human being and develop all three centers to their full potential. All external manifestations or attributes displayed by form practice are really because of the inner development of the practitioner. *Remember, for every outer manifestation there is always a corresponding inner one. Do your forms as much as possible.*

The Outer Aspect - The Law of Repetition

The body or the moving center has its own language, *the sense of self and repetition.* This is how the moving center learns and remembers. Yes, the moving center has its own memory, sometimes called muscle memory or neural memory. Repetition over a long period of time causes changes in the nervous system, both in the brain and the spinal nerves, developing new neural pathways that are the foundation of new techniques. As the neural pathways develop, the muscles that are innervated by these nerves also develop according to the attributes commensurate with execution of the technique. The Ten Thousand rule is basically a description of the amount of repetition needed to crystalize a technique into the moving center. Once this memory is crystalized, it is there for life. It becomes an automatic function. Of course, unless the technique is maintained by practice, the quality of expression will suffer because the "connections" between the centers begin deteriorate. But the muscle memory is there and will come back if the need presents itself. Once I was accosted by a man with an axe. It had been perhaps ten years since I practiced double outer-forearm blocks. Yet, as if I was an observer (see chapter on the Sparring Mind), my body leaped forward, striking his arms that swung the axe. The block broke his grip, causing the axe to fall harmlessly to the ground. As a result of the step and double outer forearm block my body came to the quarter posterior position of my attacker and I encircled his arms and pressed him to the ground in a Full Nelson. The fight was over. This lesson helped me to understand the great significance of the memory of the moving center.

The Law of Quintessence

As a chemistry major I learned the law of quintessence. This law says that if you want to extract a pure substance from a natural source like a plant, you have to use a pure solvent and perform five extractions before you get a substance with 90% purity. For example, if you wanted to extract a medicinal alkaloid from a natural plant, you would have to use a solvent and make five consecutive extractions (using pure solvent each time) in order to produce a product that was of 90% purity.

For years I practiced form by The Law of Three. This great law of the Trinity was explained to me when I took on any project. This was from one who was a mentor to me.

"Whenever you pursue any aim, always do it three times.
Do it the first time mechanically, like you do everything else in ordinary life,
that is, unconsciously. The second time do it for yourself.
The third time do it for a purpose."

This was a great help for me in form practice because I found that the first form was average, the second form was always better and the third was the best, if I was not too tired. In a tournament, in case of a tie, you may be required to do your form at least twice, so you must practice accordingly. However, my success in form competition did not approach excellence until I applied the Law of Quintessence to my practice. In my basic practice, I would do each technique in the form five times. When I practiced segments, I would do each segment five times. When I did whole form, I would do whole form five times. In this way, I found that I could refine each technique, each segment and each form to the best refinement possible (90%) and really impress the techniques into my body memory.

What was the solvent? *Mindfulness.* Mindfulness is placing your attention on the body as it functions. The more pure your mindfulness, the more the quality of the technique can be extracted. Just repetition without mindfulness gives limited results, especially in the quality of the technique. Mindfulness in martial art is the conscious directing of the body to sense the proper execution of the technique. The best way to have feedback of your mindfulness is to have the objective view of your instructor, or a video tape of your form. With this direction, your mindful practice will impress the sense of the inner attributes of the technique into your body memory.

Form Raises Your Level of Being

Your level of being is *how you are at any given moment.* Raising your level of being is the engagement of all three centers in harmony. *A higher level of being is an approach toward unity in one's self.* The following diagram conveys how form can raise your level of being.

Man approaching inner unity.

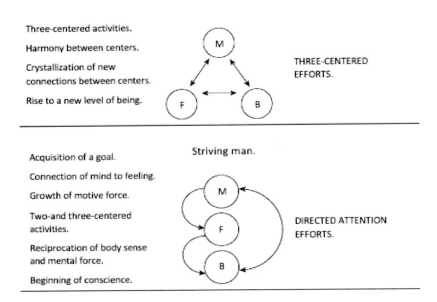

Three-centered activities.

Harmony between centers.

Crystallization of new
connections between centers.

Rise to a new level of being.

THREE-CENTERED
EFFORTS.

Striving man.

Acquisition of a goal.

Connection of mind to feeling.

Growth of motive force.

Two-and three-centered
activities.

Reciprocation of body sense
and mental force.

Beginning of conscience.

DIRECTED ATTENTION
EFFORTS.

Man as he is.

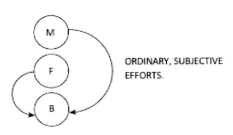

Connections formed accidentally
by life.

No connection between mind and
feeling. No motive force.

One-centered activities only.

No formulation of a goal.

Constant inner turmoil.

ORDINARY, SUBJECTIVE
EFFORTS.

M = The totality of mental functions.   F = The totality of feeling functions.

B = The totality of moving functions.

UNITY IN MAN

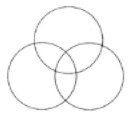

This is the goal of a real man. All three centers exist and act together in a harmonius manner. This state is the result of three-centered efforts over a long period of time. This is the beginning of *will*. This is the inner value of forms. If the practice of forms is sustained, the state of being of a man will gradually produce an inner unity. As a result of forms practice, substances of a higher level will crystalize into this unity. Gradally, these substances will *overflow* into one's ordinary life and will change the level of being of the practioner. *This is the value of forms.*

Chapter 13

I have to ask the question?
Do I answer to Life?
Do I wish to continue my life
for the opportunity of becoming Awake?
It is as if, in whatever I do,
I have introduce this question
of the purpose of my life?
Then I must constantly ask,
is this what I do now,
in conformity of reaching that purpose,
or not?

W. A. Nyland

The Link

We are living in a body. This body is an essential part of the whole of our human experience. It is not something separate.

The body is the link between the inner and the outer world, and we don't know how to use this body.

For that, these are training movements, the learning of the use of the body as a means of expression, learning the language of gesture, learning to control one's body in delicate, very difficult, and sometimes very awkward ways.

This is a great revelation!

At once, one suddenly realizes that this is a wonderful instrument, and I have never seen what it can do for me.

John J. Bennett
Gurjieff Movements

The Organ of Sense

We all know, more or less, that we have five senses. In order of their importance to us, they are vision, hearing, smell, taste and touch. As far as mechanical reception of impressions goes, vision is the most important, comprising almost 80% of our "world experience." Auditory or hearing impressions are of secondary importance, and if I had to guess, I would say sound occupies about 10% of our world. The rest of the impressions impacting us are divided among smell, taste and touch. Notice I said "mechanical" reception because there is basically no conscious effort involved with the reception of impressions. They just come in and we react to them with the impressions that are previously stored, or "pigeonholed" in our brain. When we think and talk about sense impressions we assume that they "come in" and produce an effect. That is what science says. Actually, what really happens is that *attention flows outward from our sense organs.* This outward flow of attention from the sense organs is what we *identify* with and how we attach to the world. If you could ponder a while on what you "really have" as a human being, you would realize that the only *possession of any real and lasting intrinsic value is your attention*, or at least it could be.

We have learned that if one sense organ is damaged or lost, the other senses develop beyond their previous level. For instance, a person who is blind depends so much more on hearing and touch. Therefore it is reasonable to assume that if *attention is developed and/or directed* on a sense organ, that sense will become more vivified or capable of receiving higher or finer impressions than before. I was privileged to have a blind friend, Ed Luttrup, for several years. He could distinguish people and their location in a party setting by the tone of their voice. He could read with his fingertips. He would know when someone came into the room by the movement of air over his skin. When he walked, he used the sound of his cane to place objects in the room, and he could sense the body heat of a person near him. His memory was extraordinary, for he had had sight before diabetes claimed it. He remembered places, distances and conversations in detail that had happened years ago. His friendship helped me to ponder deeply upon our sense organs, their functions, their limits, their possible development and how we use them to create our reality. Then a question arose in me. "Is that all there is to it?" Are there other organs of sense that are accessible to us that would open up and deepen the significance of our life?

My search for the answers to this question, and others, proceeded along two lines. First, since the quality and quantity of the impressions of the sense organs were dependent on the quality and quantity of my attention, then it should be a major aim for me to develop my attention. Second, since in my usual state my attention was mechanical, or *undirected*, could I develop *directed attention* to use my energy in a more conscious manner?

As I spoke about in sparring, one can develop the peripheral vision, so that impressions could bypass the fore and mid brain and go directly to the cerebellum. This would dramatically reduce your reaction time to physically respond to a threat. This development would also help us to truly *see everything in our sight*. In some esoteric groups, this is called *gazing*. There are many exercises you can practice to develop what you see. One for instance, is "quadrant vision." This is where you consciously draw a vertical and horizontal line across your visual picture and mentally note what is in each quadrant. Another is when an artist intentionally *squints their eyes* to better see the light and dark values of a landscape or subject that they are painting or drawing. Artists also use the technique of painting an object or subject upside down to achieve a more objective interpretation instead identifying with subject.

In hearing, if you close your eyes and *listen to all sounds*, you will become aware of many more sounds than usual. For me, it is amazing how little I normally hear. It is the same with smell, taste and touch. If you direct your attention toward a sense organ consciously over a long period of time, the quality and quantity impressions deepen and broaden. For instance, the sense of touch can expand to take in the force of gravity by the impression of pressure on your feet, legs, buttocks and arms if you are sitting. The sense of touch can take in pressure of the clothes on your skin and the air on the exposed skin. The sense of smell can be developed like a dog if we took time to smell every object and fragrance.

When I was a young man, I came across a form of meditation called the Three Minute Exercise. This exercise is one of directed attention on all of the senses, plus a lot more. If you are interested in opening up the world of your sense organs, and therefore your own world, I would recommend practicing this exercise for a long period of time over your life. It is listed in the chapter of this book titled Meditations..

The Sixth Sense

When you do form, you begin to direct your body to assume certain postures, including stance, chambering (starting position for blocks, kicks and strikes) and extension (or ending position). When trying to learn these body positions, you begin by putting your attention on them. Attention from the mind is sent to the body part or entire body relative to its orientation. After the attention is sent, the body part *sends back impressions to the mind in the form of a sense your position*. This is your *sense of the body existing, is the Sixth Sense*. Sometimes it is called "Self-Awareness." The impressions sent back to the mind from the body are usually mixed with all other subjective impressions and therefore overlooked as a distinct sense and ignored. However, when the instructor corrects your body position, say a stance, again and again you send this *direct attention to the body and its positional awareness*. Gradually, you get better and better at the proper posture of the stance by becoming accustomed to the tenseness and relaxation of certain muscles and the overall balance of the body. At one point in my taekwondo training I had an instructor that made me stay in each stance until my body began to shake and the pain was excruciating. The next day, I knew beyond a doubt which muscles were used in that stance because of the soreness. Soreness can be a lead into the sense of yourself existing. The "sense of the technique" becomes of paramount importance when you do jumping or spinning techniques. Only the sense of the body existing in midair gives the practitioner correct knowledge of the execution of the technique.

The dynamic of the relationship between the mind and the body looks something like this.

Attention sent from the mind ------------------------→ Body part

Reception in the mind ←------------------------------ Sense of the body part

In some esoteric schools this is called the *mind-body connection* or *mindfulness*. This is the engagement of two centers. The mind-body relationship is extremely important to the total development of the human psyche. This is one of the great potentials of human growth. This is the basic idea behind all rhythmic-movement exercises or directed-movement activities. This, in my opinion, is one of the great values we can receive when we practice martial art. I call it, *mentation by form.*

The main problem associated with the development of Sense is because in most martial art settings, the practice of this activity is incidental and begins subjectively without a clear understanding of what is happening and *how to develop it consciously!* Since it is not understood on the level of most practitioners, the importance of this activity is not placed upon the pedestal of understanding it deserves. Not only that, it is difficult to practice because *the Sense of One's Body Existing is a conscious effort of directed attention.*

It is the potential of a human being to become conscious of the body existing or Self-Consciousness. Most people assume they are already conscious of themselves, including their body. Nothing could be farther from the truth. Right now, reading this book, are you conscious of your body existing? Is there a Sense of your body existing? No. The fact is that your mind was totally identified with reading and totally unconscious of your body. It is like this every second of every day of your life. There is little or no mind-body relationship. You have to admit that there is little or no connection between your mind and body. This must be developed!

If you can conceive of the senses as the receptors of impressions, then impressions become a sort of food for the mind. In fact, our awareness is totally supported by impressions. Without impressions we would cease to exist instantly. Solid and liquid food and air are combined with impressions of the mind to produce the totality of nourishment for the human body. You can live for forty to sixty days without solid food, but only three to four minutes without air. You cannot live for one second without impressions. I remember reading an experiment called *Sensory Deprivation* that took place in the 1970s. A person was placed in a wet suit, with all of the skin covered. Special gloves were placed over the hands so the fingers could not register touch. The ears were plugged so that no sounds were heard. The eyes were sealed with patches so no light could enter. Then the person was immersed in a large pool of water warmed to exactly 98.6 degrees and suspended so that there was no gravitational force on the body. Air was made available with a small mask over the mouth and nose. Once the participant was totally deprived of impressions, the experimenters noted the time and watched. The experimenters observed that within minutes the participants began to flail and flounder with uncoordinated movements. When interviewed afterward, the participants all said they began to hallucinate and *lost all sense of identity and time.* Some became horrified or frightened but none of them had the sense that they were moving or had a body. It was an out-of-body experience. The only thing that remained was pure consciousness. This experiment left a deep impression on me, so that in the years to come I was drawn to the question, *what is the sense and significance of my life?*

Because of my association with certain esoteric groups, I found that the development of the Sixth Sense was an important aspect in the growth of myself as a human being. So important was this inner aspect, I found that there was a special exercise from ancient times that one could practice in the form of a meditation. The *Sensing Exercise* is in the Meditations chapter of this book. In addition, it became apparent to me that consciously directed bodily movements in the form of sacred dances required the Organ of Sense to participate in the body existing in harmony with the growth of one's feelings and awareness. It was these movements I participated in for many years. No other place on earth do these movements exist except in these groups.

When I was no longer in these groups, I looked for similar types of mind-body exercises and was attracted to some types of martial art, specifically forms. It was quite a letdown to find that the practitioners of martial art had no knowledge of the Sixth Sense, or the importance of its development other than incidentally. Others practiced for the exoteric values, I practiced for the inner aspect. You can too.

The practice of form and the sense of the body existing is like the tip of the ice berg. The main significance of the ice berg is hidden by water. The main significance of form, is hidden in unconsciousness. The practice of form *is a type of meditation or directing consciousness inward.* To augment the development of the Sixth Sense, other forms of meditation should be practiced. This creates a type of reinforcing exercise that helps you develop an objective view of the body and a distinct separation of awareness. I came across three separate mediations that can be of tremendous value to a martial art practitioner and truly open up the inner aspect. The first one is called *The Three Minute Exercise,* the second is called *The Draining Exercise* and the third is called *The Sensing Exercise*. Form practice and any or all of the meditations develop and work with the finer energies necessary to open one up to higher influences.

Acknowledgement of Higher Energies

The eastern concept of an invisible energy is called Chi. Chi is flowing through the body and somehow animates it. Chi energy is the major theme in Chinese medicine. The aura of living creatures is a central theme in yoga. Electromagnetic forces are acknowledged in modern science through electrical potentials measured across the skin, like the polygraph. Modern imagery can see the electromagnetic forces activating areas in the brain. Meditation has been shown to affect these areas in specific ways. Kirlian photography shows images of energy even when parts of the physical body have been amputated. Even the piezoelectric touch screen of your phone exposes this energy.

The idea of *higher energies* interpenetrating the physical body is difficult to understand by people who only believe in what the five senses give them. Yet they accept radio waves, electricity, magnetism and gravity.

For me this idea of higher energies was developed in this way. If we accept the fact that atoms are the building blocks of matter, then we also know there are spaces in between the atoms. In fact, the spaces in between atoms are gigantic compared to the atoms themselves. If we take ice as an example, we know that ice is a solid form of water and the spaces between molecules are close, causing the state of water to become a solid. If the ice melts, we see that the spaces between the atoms increase, allowing the atoms to flow over each other and become liquid. Again, if water evaporates or becomes steam, the spaces between the molecules increase even more, allowing water to be a gas. We cannot see the gas except in the form of a cloud, yet it is still water and has energy and force. As the density of matter decreases, at some point matter is inaccessible to our sense organs, yet it still has mass and force.

In between these spaces, we know that ionized atoms create electromagnetic fields that interpenetrate matter and have aligning forces on matter. This is called a bioelectric field. The coursing of blood through the arteries, the enervation of nerves and muscles all cause the influx of electromagnetic fields that define the form of the body. Sharks have sense organs called the ampulla of Lorenzini. This sense organ in the shark can actually "see" the electromagnetic form of their prey as a visual experience. Sharks can locate and catch seals by seeing their bioelectric field.

The concentration (like a battery) and manipulation of these forces have been practiced in martial art for millennia. It is called Qi Quong. These forces can harden the body and be projected beyond the body to affect matter. Some people say that the act of breaking boards is not a physical one but a psychological one. Think about it.

You would do well to strive to understand the Organ of Sense and how to develop this force inside yourself.

Chapter 14

*Learn to separate
the fine from the coarse.*

The Emerald Tablets of Hermes Trismegistus

The Role of Music in Martial Art

When I was in college, trying to find the answers to the questions that were bothering me, I began by studying psychology. At a certain point, I became disillusioned watching and listening to the people around me in class. It became clear to me that most of their exposition was "mental ejaculation." Then I took a course in physiological psychology, and a new world opened for me. I realized that much of psychology had a biological basis. I left psychology and went into biology. Soon after that, I realized that all of biology was based on chemistry, so I went into chemistry. Then I realized that in order to understand chemistry I needed to know physics, but I found that physics is nothing but math. To make a long story short, I ended up with a double major, biology and chemistry, and a double minor, math and psychology. I still did not find the answers to my questions about life.

Looking back, it almost seemed that every aspect of science was like an onion, starting with sociology as the outer layer. Like concentric spheres, each layer is supported by an inner layer. Each layer is influenced by the layer above and the layer below. The process of my schooling consisted of peeling back a layer at a time to try to fathom the inner truth upon which all layers depended. I did not know it then, but this "science onion" was an expression of the Law of Octaves.

The conclusion of my search in science ended in what was then a controversy in quantum physics. Which explanation fit the visible universe the best, a particle theory or wave theory? Quantum physics found that the best explanation of universe was *waves of packets of energy* that could act as matter or vibrational force. Gravitational waves, electromagnetic waves, sound waves, ocean waves, brain waves and all forms of energy are transformed into packets of energy that are constantly transmuting themselves into whatever medium they pass. Another way to look at it is through the concept of periods. Every independent cosmic concentration has a beginning and end. That end is another beginning. Waves are the periodic table of all things. The high and low of all things blend into the middle. It is The Law of Three Forces. Day and night, waking and sleeping, going out into the world and coming home, breathing in and out, the heart contracting and relaxing, the flicker fusion rate of visual impressions and the planets circling the sun are all examples of waves of energy manifesting in a periodic motion.

How does this relate to martial art? Each technique has a beginning and end, blending together to strike or block. Each form begins and ends in the same place with the expression of the form in the middle. In sparring the plyometric vibration rate is increased. This periodic motion either ascends or descends by means of its vibration rate, or how close the periods repeat. A higher vibration rate means higher energy or finer vibrations. A lower vibration rate means lower energy or grosser vibrations. The force that creates the magnitude of a vibration rate is the force that originates the *Do* of the vibration and is called the impulse or impetus. This relates to the explosiveness, power and acceleration of the technique.

With all this being said, now look at a man. He is three-centered being with a body, a feeling center and an intellectual center. As we spoke about forms before, the aim of forms is to combine the three centers into one. This is a higher level of being. This is an enthalpy (concentration of energy or force) or Qi Quong. The mind is the director, the feelings the motivator and the body the executioner, all acting in a harmonic manner. This manifestation in form shows us what could be the possible development of a person in outer life. The more and more we practice form, the more a certain residue of this harmony spills over into our ordinary life, and we become a more harmonious man.

In esoteric circles, musical choreography of forms or movements are designed to affect the feelings in a specific manner. It allows them to congeal into a real emotion that could be centered in the heart. This emotion, when fully functional, is able to have intuitional understanding beyond anything the intellect can access. The practice of these esoteric movements were designed to transmute the multitude of small feelings that are spread out over the various nerve plexuses of the body into a real functioning center of emotion that migrates to the heart. Gradually, four real higher functions of the heart will begin to appear. These are inspiration, aspiration, silence and conscience. Although I have never seen it in the martial art I have practiced, I am sure that sometime in the past there were esoteric martial arts that understood the significance of musical tones and their place in forms. This was the reason for their special choreography in each specific form. It is to transmit esoteric knowledge to generations yet unborn in a manner that cannot be misinterpreted by the intellect.

In the martial art system I participated in, we did have music in forms. It was a competition called Creative Forms. Here you made up your own form and then performed it to the music of your choice. The music was usually borrowed from a contemporary song a person liked and they tried to match their form to the rhythm of the music. Sometimes there was good rhythm and movement and sometimes there was just noise with movement. I made up my own musical form also. However, there was no understanding as to the real reason for the blending of the movement and the music. It was just more or less a kind of subjective dance to the music.

I know that what I have said is difficult to understand unless you have actually practiced esoteric or sacred dance, but I have. I wanted you to be aware of what might be possible for martial art, what some martial art probably was and perhaps may still be in some remote ancient monastery.

Now, on a more practical note, you must understand that feelings are so intimately joined to the body that the arousal of any feeling immediately is manifested in body posture, movement, gesture, facial expression or tone of voice. You can use this understanding to arouse the body to a higher intensity in your workouts. For instance, I have always used music to raise my sparring class to a higher level. Using music with a fast beat causes the body to adapt to that beat. Most of my students did not know that they needed to bounce during their sparring to increase their explosiveness. By sparring to an increased rate of vibration, the mind begins to shut down and the body can follow the beat of the music. The higher the vibration rate, the more the mind is shut down and the natural speed of the body is elevated accordingly. I have found that not only is the quality of sparring elevated, but the attitude of the entire class is raised. They really have a great time with the proper music. *Music is the great motivator.*

Music is also of value in your practice, whether it be forms, sparring or bag work. If you do competition, you know that class time is not enough practice. You must practice on your own. For me, it took about four hours a week of extra practice just to compete, and that was in addition to my regular classes. Many, many times I would have to drag myself out to my dojang to be true to my aim to become World Champion. Yet once I turned on the music I had recorded to practice by, my mood, my intent and my aim sprang alive. My workouts were more intense, more fun and more satisfying. As a result, my efforts were rewarded accordingly in the ring.

Add music to your training.

Listening to Music

Music is the great enlivening force of life. It is everywhere, in everything, on every level, from the galactic spirals to the nucleus of the atom. Science has even found that several planets in our solar system, including Earth, are emitting electromagnetic "music" that can be recorded and converted into sounds that we can hear. The Law of Octaves is the DNA (blueprint) of the universe. When you study the universe, you study yourself. When you study yourself, you study the universe. The great Hermes Trismegistus aphorism states, *As above, So below.* Martial art is an esoteric study of one's self. When you speak of music, you must speak of the sense organs. The eye is the sense organ for the music of the visible spectrum of light. The ear is the sense organ for the music of the vibration of the atmosphere. The organs of smell and taste are known to light up seven different areas in the brain. If they were more developed, a recognition of their octaves would be revealed. The Organ of Sense is the receptor of the music of body vibrations.

In actuality, the entire nervous system is a musical string. I found two exercises that helped me to experience the octaves of the world inside myself.

The first was the Three Minute Exercise. This exercise is, among other things, a study of the sense organs and a way to vivify and bring into consciousness all the senses, including sounds. The second exercise was that of experiencing the nervous system as a tuning fork.

Sit comfortably with your spine erect but relaxed. Close your eyes and listen to music without words. Visualize your spine as a long string. As you listen to the music, sense where the tones of the music fall onto your spine. Select a piece of music that is relatively simple with only a few tones. You will sense that each tone falls on or activates a specific place in your spine. Higher tones will fall higher on your spine, perhaps in the neck or throat area. Lower tones stimulate corresponding lower places on your spine. Very high notes will activate places in your brain. Once you understand and practice this, you will notice that the music actually stimulates that area of the spine to vibrate. When you are more adapt at this exercise, you will notice that the vibrations of certain areas of the spine actually cause your solar plexus to vibrate. Now you can experience how music can stimulate real emotion coming from your heart. It is the same with higher and lower vibrations and their effect on the mind and the body. Certain vibrations energize the body, and certain vibrations create emotional effects. *Other vibrations shut down thought and open up awareness.*

It has always been my wish, because of the lack of music in our forms, that perhaps a person reading this who has musical ability could develop a musical form based on the actual postures and moves (stances, guard, blocks, strikes, reverses, jumps, spins and combinations thereof) of each existing form. Every single move or posture could have a single note or chord. Although subjective, at least the emotional force of music could drive the experience of forms into a deeper level of being. If there is anyone reading this who has this ability, I ask for your help to develop this emotional level of your form. If you do, please allow me to participate in that form.

Many esoteric teachings have understood this relationship on how music affects a person inwardly to transform states of mind, body and feeling into a harmonious function that can raise one's level of being and open one up to higher influences. For me, my understanding and participation of sacred movements with music is one of the most liberating activities I have ever experienced. I feel that sometime in the past, martial art was practiced with this knowledge.

I leave you with one aphorism.

Do not listen to music with your mind, let it come in and go to where it belongs. Let it penetrate as deep as it can go.

Chapter 15

I believe that a man's greatest hour, his finest fulfillment,
is in the moment when he has worked his heart out
in a good cause, and lies exhausted on the field of battle.
He is exhausted but victorious.
The value of all of our daily efforts
is greater and more enduring if they create
in each one of us,
a person who grows and understands
and really lives.
It is one who prevails for a larger and more
meaningful victory,
not only in time, but hopefully
in all eternity.

Vince Lombardi

Tournament Preparation

At some point in your martial art journey, you will become exposed to tournaments. Tournaments are an important part of martial art. They are the platform whereby you can objectify your level of being in relation to other practitioners. In your mind, you always think that you are better than you really are. In order to close the distance between what you think and what you do, competition is a must. Much of this book is written for those who *wish to compete*. The principles espoused in this book are the same for anyone in martial art, whether they compete or not. However the depth of understanding of these principles cannot be accessed until one has tournament experience and a drive to *find out what it really takes to be a World Champion*.

I remember that I had no wish to go to tournaments until I was a purple belt. Then my classmates told me I should go, especially one young lady Susan Menchaca, who was herself a World Champion. I remember that after sparring her once, she told me, "You should compete. If you do, you will wipe them all out." So I went. I was terrified that I would have to fight someone I didn't even know. I am sure that my sparring opponent was just as afraid as I, for he could not contain himself. When the order "fight" was given, he came at me with a number three side kick. I entered the "zone" for the first time. Everything slowed down. I saw a foot appear in front of me crashing into his jaw. It was my foot extending from my side kick. It knocked him out.

After that, I embarked on twenty-plus years of tournament competition. During that time I was awarded thirty-one Top Ten medals, won fifteen World Titles and achieved the coveted Quadruple Crown. I competed in forms, sparring, weapons and combat weapons. Why did I compete? In my mind, a thought process took shape that went something like this.

1. What does it *really take* to become a World Champion?

2. I think that I am *pretty good*. Can I prove it?

3. Tournaments are instruments that compress all of the difficulties of life into a very short period of time. If I could participate in events

like this and succeed, then I could take on any difficulty in ordinary life and prosper. I could stuff years of regular living into one year of extraordinary life.

4. I could practice the esoteric principles that I was exposed to in my early life. I could raise my level of being.

5. I wanted to be an example for my kids. I wanted to show them that they could be anything they wanted if they gave dedicated effort over a long period of time.

6. I wanted to overcome all of my fears.

If you are motivated by any of these things, then this chapter is for your dream.

Types of Fighters

Although tournament sparring seems wild and unorganized at first sight, it is really a mental, strategic dance that takes a lot of preparation. Strategy is of utmost importance after physical excellence. Strategy also changes as the level of your competition rises. One of my instructors, Mrs. Kathleen Flatt, first introduced me to the use of strategy in sparring. Most fighters learn what their strengths are and arrange their strategy around them. The foremost strengths are the physical attributes, height, physique, flexibility, speed and age. Tall people usually rely on kicking. Strong people with powerful physiques are usually aggressive. Flexible people excel in kicking and combinations. Shorter people must rely upon speed, movement and punching and are usually defensive fighters. The age brackets for ATA tournaments are usually in ten year spans for older people. For instance, 50-59 years, except for the oldest bracket of 60-99 years. Age makes a great difference within the bracket. "Young people," just coming into a bracket, have a distinct advantage over older people that have been in that age group for several years.

You can divide these classes of fighters again into offensive or defensive fighters. Then again you can divide them by the primary techniques that a fighter uses. Most fighters use the technique that they have had the most success with and use it over and over again. However, there is an interesting and important weakness in people that fight the same way all the time. Since they are very successful with a single technique, they rarely practice any other techniques and thereby when their main technique is thwarted in the ring they don't know what to do. A lot of their strategy comes from their rank training. Generally speaking, a First Degree Black Belt must have one really good technique to win a lot. However, a Second or Third Degree Black Belt must have two or more really good techniques to win a lot. At Fourth Degree, Fifth Degree and beyond, a fighter must *be really good at all sparring techniques to win constantly*. At this level of competition you will see really good interactive sparring, for the strategies of less-experienced fighters do not reach this level.

The Amazon

This type of fighter is usually blessed with a great physique, is very flexible and very strong. They are able to deliver a kick to the head many times without putting their foot down, advancing toward you with each kick. The preferred kick is the number one round kick. This type of fighter is very common in the women's ring, hence the name. They come at you with force.

It usually does you no good to stand there and try to block all the kicks, for as soon as you block, you are open somewhere and eventually will get your noggin clocked. If you happen to be just as capable as the Amazon, then a battle royal ensues for who has the better, more powerful technique and the most stamina. If you are smaller and less flexible, only two strategies exist for you against this fighter.

The first is that you must always fight in a closed stance relative to the Amazon. Every time the fighter comes for you, you must do a reverse side kick, reverse hook kick or reverse heel kick followed by punches. The weakness of the number one round kick is when the kick is fully extended or being pulled back into a chamber. The chest/belly target area is exposed, especially at the belt level. For me, a *reverse hooking side kick* was perfect. You must be careful when executing this kick, for many Amazons have the ability to still kick you in the head as you are turning. You must "lay down" in your reverse to avoid this.

The second, is to fight in an open stance and constantly V-out, block and punch. This makes the Amazon constantly kick and turn, causing them to lose the power in their technique, disturb their balance and expose their open chest/belly target area. I have seen this many times. I remember one match between an Amazon, who could stick her leg straight up into the atmosphere above her head, and a small lady, my mentor Susan Menchaca. Mrs. Menchaca was a very fast, maneuverable and an aggressive counter puncher. My mentor won.

There is a modification to the V-out counter technique. Instead of V-out, block, punch; it is V-out, block, side kick or jump round kick. If you prefer this technique, you must practice a great deal, for it *requires precise timing.*

The Turtle

This was one of the most difficult of fighters for me. The Turtle is one who leans way back, to get their head out of range, and sidekicks. At the same time they cover their chest/belly target area. They always keep their body turned sideways, and their sidekick is more like a semi back-kick. They always back up a step after each kick, then go back into their shell and waits for you to come in on them. Their front leg (kicking leg) has little weight on it, allowing them to kick quickly and repeat kick. They advance on you with small sliding steps, always ready to kick and always turning to keep you sideways to their body. It is very difficult to find a target area.

After some failures when engaging these fighters, I finally hit on a strategy that worked. Staying in an open stance, I bounced around in a circle, just out of range, causing them to constantly reset. When I saw that they were not quite set I feinted toward them, drawing them out, causing an unbalanced kick, then veer out to their open side and counter with a jump round kick, punch, and punch. Even if my kick did not score, follow-up punches usually did, for their target the area was exposed.

One of my best opponents, Mr. Mike Samples, had a style similar to this. However, in addition to his excellent side kick, he had a devastating hook kick and lightning round kick. If you got by all of these, a counter punch was waiting for you if you came down too close after a short kick. If all of that failed, he had a jump back kick that would catch you if you tried to come in to punch. He was truly a great fighter and I felt extremely fortunate to finally beat him and another great adversary of mine, Mr. Peter

Robustelli, on the same day. Mr. Robustelli was tall, powerful, flexible and aggressive and he always pressed you. He could kick you in the head with all of his techniques and had a reverse heel kick that could take your head off. You can only rise to the level of your competition. I had the best.

The Runner

I am not sure why this type of person would want to do tournament sparring, but they can be very frustrating to fight. Every time you would advance toward them, or kick they would take a step back. No matter what you did they would then step back without counter punching or kicking. Eventually, you would get really frustrated and sloppy, then throw caution to the wind and come in hard on them. When you put your foot down, then they would counter punch you.

After trying the Whirling Dervish on them several times, I could hear my wife Sherry calling, "Jimmy, that is not working!" Finally I hit on it. Gradually, I would work them into the corner of the ring with sidekicks, until they were on the edge of the ring or with a foot out of bounds, *then I would come after them*, knowing that they could not score nor did they have anyplace to run. I got many points because they were out of bounds and could not score.

The Whirling Dervish or Blitzkrieg

This technique was made famous by Chuck Norris. I watched many of his fights on video, and once the bell rang he leaped forward with kick after kick after punch until he literally ran his opponent out of the ring. His onslaught was so aggressive, powerful and unrelenting that it caught his opponent off balance and overwhelmed them. It usually began with a skipping side kick, number two round kick, reverse side kick, punch, punch, then jump reverse side kick or heel kick. The key to his assault was a powerful skipping side kick that got his opponent moving backward, then unrelenting kicks and punches as a follow-up. One aspect of this style that is important is that if the judges see punches landing at the same time, they usually give the point to the fighter moving forward. *Remember that.*

There are several ways to defend against this type of fighter. The first is the *Stop Hit*, made famous by Bruce Lee. When your opponent advances, you must side kick hard as they put their lead foot down to advance. If done correctly you will stop the first technique before it gets started, hence the term Stop Hit. If done precisely at the right moment with the opponent starting to elevate, they will crash to the ground from the side kick meeting their abdomen in midair. Ah, it is a beautiful thing for you and a rude awakening for them.

If this fails then a well-placed step back, side kick, reverse side kick or #2 push kick usually worked. You must be fearless with your side-kick for he is coming in for you and even if you both kick at the same time it will upset his charge. You may be very sore for a few days afterward, but you must be willing to sacrifice. I remember several times I got rebounded out of the ring by *kicking off the belly* of this powerful adversary when he bore in. The point was always mine because my chamber was above the belt.

And the last way of course, is veering out and side kicking, hook punching or a jump round kick.

The Counter Fighter

Counter fighters are pure defensive fighters. They are usually "vertically challenged," but very quick, intelligent and confident, with no qualms about "living on the edge." They press you to make you do something, hopefully a kick, and if you miss and put your front foot down, they charge in for the kill. Usually, they have lightning hands and excellent boxing skills. They might even practice Bruce Lee's, *The Tao of Jeet Kune Do: The Way of the Intercepting Fist.* If they do, watch out! They wait for your weakness to open up and then they strike. They are some of the most capable and formidable fighters you can face. In addition, when it is a tie, with no time left and next point wins, they excel. There is a general rule for competition in "sudden death" - *the first person that does something, loses.*

To "counter the counter fighter," you must understand their strategy and develop your strategy and techniques to the level that will defeat them. I fought many counter fighters, but I never lost to one, because I developed my kicking techniques to keep them away and to be faster than their counters. Some of them were perennial World Champions in forms and weapon form. I was the one that frustrated their visions for the coveted Triple Crown, before there was a Quadruple Crown.

There are two basic premises for sparring a counter fighter. The first is to develop your side kick technique to be a very high level. The second is to draw them out with a feint. *Remember, you fight like you practice.*

First you must develop your side kick to the point of devastating speed. Second, you must *chamber before and after your kick.* If you chamber before you kick, you can push the counter fighter off of you, and sometimes a judge will give you a point if you have time to extend it somewhat. Next, you must rechamber to kick again or to protect yourself and retain your balance. Also, practice your side kick-hook kick-round kick combination until it becomes body memory and leads you into *The Zone.* You stop them with the side kick, when they block downward, then you give them a head shot with the hook kick. If you score fine, if they lean their head back to avoid the hook kick, wait for them to come back at you, for they are now committed to come in. That is when you round kick them in the head. Finally, evade back and away at forty-five degrees. They are usually so committed that they blow right past you and you can reset, or reverse.

Second, you know that they are just waiting for you to do something so they can counter. As soon as you commit to an offensive move, they simply evade or block and then counter when you are rechambering, putting your foot down or off-balance. The trick is to draw them out with a feint of some sort, like a half-hearted kick, a quick step forward or a torso feint. Knowing that they will immediately counter, usually with a punch, you can be ready with your side kick.

Preparation for an Event

As you found out in the chapter on The Law of Effort, the Law of Octaves is never static. All independent cosmic concentrations, of which you are one, are either evolving or involving. This developing or retarding phenomenon is not a smooth one, it proceeds in pulses. Your training consists of individual classes or sessions. When your sessions are closer together, or more intense than the previous one, then it could be said that you are evolving. Each session makes changes in the body, mind and feelings not only after that workout, but lays the foundation for future changes if the training is continued on a regular basis. It is as if the body realizes that you want it to do more of this training *when each session creates adaptations that develop a higher level of skill.* If you do the same type of training over and over again however, the adaptation plateaus and the growth ceases. Then the training must change in character in order to continue to develop beyond this plateau. Remember the Fa Bridge, remember the Si Do? Remember the Super Effort?

If you only compete in one event, the training necessary to grow is not comparatively that difficult, for it follows a geometric curve. However, if you compete in two or more events, your efforts are compounded commensurate with the number of events. Because each event requires different qualities within each technique, the muscles, tendons, ligaments and nervous system must develop each quality necessary to excel in that event. For instance, the qualities needed for sparring are different than the qualities needed for forms, therefore you must train to develop all the qualities needed for each event. This is quite an undertaking.

Generally speaking, however, there are certain athletic qualities that you must continuously maintain in order to have a good base to excel in the more difficult techniques. After much reading on the subject and much experimentation, I developed a training cycle that would peak right before the tournament. I would go into the ring at my highest level of being. Here is the training cycle I developed.

1. For a full week after a tournament, I would rest my body. I would not train or go to class. Then I would begin my light, passive stretching routine. If I had video of the tournament, I would watch it and note my weaknesses and strengths. I would also note the strategy of my opponents.

2. After resting for a week, I would begin basic weight training with light weights and high repetition twice a week to gain my strength back, with stretching afterward. Next, I would do speed drills to maintain my fast twitch fibers. For form, both regular and weapons, I would concentrate on individual techniques I identified as weaknesses in the videos. This phase would last two to three weeks. Also, I would do single techniques with combat weapons.

3. In phase three I would stop the weights and continue my stretching. I choreographed my sparring moves on the bag that I would be

using according to the opponents strategy I observed in the video. I would do the same with combat weapons. In forms, both regular and weapons, I would begin doing segments only. Usually, I would follow the Law of Quintessence, with five repetitions of each segment.

4. In phase four I would begin plyometric workouts once a week to maintain my explosiveness. I would reduce my form and weapon form training to three repetitions of each segment. I would stop the choreographing of sparring and combat weapon sparring and go to sparring class regularly.

5. Phase five would begin two to three weeks before the tournament. Here is when I would cease plyometric training and begin form work in earnest. I would do the entire form three times. I would do each form in a different direction to prevent visual accustoming and drive the movements into my muscle memory. The very last week before the tournament I would rest my body totally and do visual imagery of my forms and choreographed sparring moves. I would also visualize myself smiling and happy, standing on the podium as a World Champion with the gold metals around my neck.

Nervousness

It is sometimes said that one year in martial art is equivalent to two years of ordinary life. The logic behind this statement is that a tournament competitor has many more life experiences when he competes, and these experiences are much more intense. The tournament ring is a crucible of stresses that most people try to avoid. Knowing that you will go into the ring and expose yourself and your manifestations to other people can be quite disconcerting and sometimes border on panic-inducing. Your self-love fears that you will expose your inability and worry that people will see that you are not the person *you think you are*. All of the subjective manifestations of the mind and the feelings seem to come out prior to this contest. *The mind always wants to know the outcome of an event before the event even takes place.* Then the mind tries to visualize the event literally as a hallucination and the feelings get drawn into the inner chaos that follows. The body reacts by secreting adrenaline, causing the breathing to become shallow, the mouth dry, the palms sweaty, and the solar plexus explodes and radiates out the extreme feeling of fight-or-flight. You are high as a kite on adrenaline. This cycle can even reach panic proportions before you enter into the ring. The anticipation of this future event will produce nervousness, anxiety and even fear. It can be quite devastating to some people. Even the thought that you are actually going to *fight another person* can initiate this internal dialog.

I struggled for years with this *Anticipatory Aspect of the Associative Process*. Here is how I dealt with it over the years as a gradual realization and the practice of non-identifying. Although it never went away, it does not have the debilitating effect on me that it once did. I have gained more self-control, and my level of being has been raised.

1. Realizing that this was a hallucination that was happening *and acknowledging it for what it is, and trying not to indulge in it or identify with it.*

2. I had to see it as an internal process of mine that had no bearing on reality. It was a hallucination.

3. I understood that this was a *negative state and was being fed by my inner subjectivity.*

4. The only way to free myself from this state was not to indulge in it or feed it. *The main effort was to not express the physical symptoms.*

5. I had a great epiphany - *everything that I think about and feel before I go into the ring, and after I leave the ring, has no value about what happens in the ring.*

6. *Realizing that the only thing of real intrinsic value inside the ring was my training.*

7. Finally, I realized that if I could train every possible time that was allotted to me before the tournament and train to best level I could, *then I would know that I had done everything possible to prepare for the tournament. I could step into the ring with acceptance of myself, my striving and whatever the outcome that was the result. I would be at peace. I was now.*

Chapter 16

*The Spirit of the Thing
is You.*

**Miyamoto Musashi
The Book of Five Rings**

Meditations

Meditation can be a very nebulous undertaking without understanding what the goal is or the reasoning behind it. There is also much disinformation and misinformation surrounding its practice. There are literally scores of meditative processes out there from all types of sources. Science has justified meditation as a healthy practice with many benefits – the reduction of stress and anxiety, the increase of mental clarity and focus, the reduction of blood pressure, the increase of attention span and the development of awareness.

During my esoteric search, I came across several meditations. I have settled on only four that have value for me and that have helped me in the development of my martial art goals.

1. Visualization.

2. The Three Minute Exercise.

3. The Draining Exercise.

4. The Sensing Exercise.

Visualization

This meditation is of great value in the improvement of your form, of sparring choreography and positively effecting the future of outcome of your tournament competition.

Sit quietly in room or space so that you will not be disturbed. Close your eyes and relax your body. Let the busy thoughts of the day die down. Begin to *visualize yourself doing your form* as perfectly as possible. See and experience every stance, block and strike. Do not be in a hurry but have a perfect vision of the form from the beginning to the end. Many times during this process you will lose your attention. Other thoughts will come in, daydreams will manifest and you may even go to sleep. When this happens, simply go back to where you left off and continue until the end of the form. It takes time and practice to develop this powerful mental tool. Without a clear aim you will have no direction for your physical efforts.

The best time to do this meditation is right after waking up in the morning and just before going to bed. These times are known as the *twilights of consciousness*. It is at these times that your internal dialog is minimal and you are more open to the conscious influences trying to reach you. As a result, these influences can penetrate deeper inside of you and find places where there is a corresponding need for them.

In the morning, right after you awake, the engine of the associative process has not yet gained momentum. Similarly at night, right before bed time the subjective processes are winding down from the day and a certain quietness results. I remember clearly one of my mentors saying to me, "If you want to change your life, read a good book right before bed time and right after waking up each morning. *Read a Good Book.*" These times correspond exactly to the twilight of the morning and the evening. These are the best times for meditation.

Use this same type of meditation with your sparring moves, both defensive and offensive.

Use this same type of meditation to positively effect the outcome of your upcoming tournament. Visualize yourself happy with a big smile, holding a Gold Medal and that huge trophy you have worked so hard for. It works!

Whether you understand this or not it is true. Negative thoughts are transmitted to other people. Positive thoughts are also transmitted to other people. If you want to help another person who is sick, injured or in a difficult situation, visualize them or their faces. Visualize them as happy, smiling and full of laughter, doing what they love the most in their life.

Visualization is a powerful meditation.

The Three Minute Exercise

Sit quietly.

Allow the busy thoughts of the day die down.

Begin to sense the weight of your body on the chair and on the floor.

Then sense the clothes that touch your body.

Sense the parts of your body that are exposed to the air.

Gaze in front of you and take in everything that is within your sight.

Hear all sounds.

Smell.

Taste.

Now open yourself up to everything that is around you.

Try to hold all of this for a few minutes.

This simple meditation can be practiced anywhere and at any time. Not only is it a study of your senses, but it also is a practice of attention. Immediately you will find that the envelope of your attention very small. You are bound by your lack of attention. Practice, practice, and practice.

The Draining Exercise

Like all the other meditations, find a comfortable space where you will not be disturbed. Sit quietly for a few minutes and relax your body. Have your feet on the floor and let your arms dangle to the side or resting on a chair.

Come to yourself. Close your eyes. Imagine that your body is filled with water. Begin at the top of your head and allow the water to drain out through your toes and fingers. Like in the bathtub, s-l-o-w-l-y allow the sense of the water level to gradually drain your head. From the crown of your head, let the level drain the forehead and all the thoughts in it. Continue to drain down through your eye sockets and then down through your nasal passages, throat and ears. As the level passes down your face allow all the face muscles to relax. When you get to the level of the jaw and throat, relax the jaw muscles and the muscles of your neck. As a result, your jaw will hang down and your mouth may slightly open. Go slowly, do not get in a hurry.

Resume the draining of the water from the neck down and across your shoulders. Sometimes this may be a little difficult. Let the tenseness in your shoulders relax. Down and down the level goes – through the chest and upper arms and then your abdomen the lower arms. At this point you may experience the energy exiting your fingertips as it flows out of your body. Let it flow.

Pick up where you left off – down the abdomen, forearms and hands, through your pelvis and sex organs, buttocks, and hips. As it drains down your thighs, hamstrings, knees and calves you will sense this energy flowing out your toes. Finish by allowing the energy to flow completely out of your feet and toes.

At this point you may experience a "hollowness" or "wholeness." There should be no thoughts, no feelings and no tenseness. You are nothing but a lump of flesh. This is your goal, try to reduce the superfluous energy in yourself. Stay in this state as long as possible. *This is your being.*

While you are draining, you may notice that your thoughts come back in or tenseness develops in an area that you have already passed. Just go back up to the top of your head and begin again. Remember, this is an exercise and you must practice it many times before you can consciously relax the entire body, mind and feelings.

The reason for this exercise is manifold. Your body is an energy factory, but much of this energy is uselessly wasted with mechanical thoughts, feelings and unnecessary muscular tension. Being aware of this tension in the body is necessary in order to conserve this energy to do useful work. In martial art it is important that you use only enough energy to perform the precise technique that is required. Unnecessary tenseness causes jerky and unbalanced movement. Tightness in the muscles reduces the speed of your techniques. Over-reaction from tense muscles causes fatigue and may contribute to injury.

You can make this exercise a daily meditation to prepare yourself for the Sensing Exercise. Or you can practice during the day whenever and wherever you find unnecessary muscular tension. Just stop and relax that area. Many people find that they have certain muscles that never relax, leading to headache, cramping and fatigue. Long term "senile postures" like slumping of the back cause certain muscles constantly contract and can crystalize the body in certain postures. Joint injury of the hip, knee and ankle can cause muscular compensation to avoid pain. This shift in the muscular tension can result in a limping or shuffling gait. It is a simple way to raise your level of being, conserve energy and have more self-control. *Relaxed readiness is what you need in martial art.*

The Sensing Exercise

After draining the body of its superfluous energy and being totally relaxed is the best time to practice the Sensing Exercise. Keep your eyes closed.

Begin by sensing your head as a whole, its form. Sense your head, your eyes, your nose, your mouth, your jaw and neck.

After you have established a sense of your head, let your attention pass to your right arm. Let your attention flow into your arm – take in the shoulder, the upper arm, the elbow, the forearm, the wrist, the hand and the fingers. The attention can be in the form of a searchlight, slowly moving over and through the totality of your arm. It is your mind sending out a certain form of energy similar to the experience of the energy flowing out your fingertips and toes during the Draining Exercise. The arm is receiving this energy in the form of a *sense of itself existing*. The mind is registering this sense of your arm existing in a special area of your brain that has had little or no activity in your life. This area of the mind is basically unused. It may be difficult at first to understand what this sense is. Do not expect any particular sensation. Once the connection is made it will become apparent. Accept whatever is there. As you continue to sense your arm, try to concentrate all of your attention on the arm, excluding everything else. At a certain point you may experience tenseness in your arm. If you do, simply relax your arm and allow the energy to flow in like osmosis. *Pretend that the arm is porous and is absorbing this energy like a sponge.* You could have a visual image of your arm or you could experience your arm as a "charged particle," existing on its own. Try to hold on to this sense of your arm existing as long as you can. Do not categorize any result you might have, just continue to sense your arm until you absolutely cannot do it any longer. Remember the essence of plyometric drills? Sense your arm until you cannot do it anymore.

When you cannot sense your arm any longer, bring all of your attention that was on your arm back to your head and sense the shape and form of your head again. When the energy is back in your head again, then try to sense your right leg. Sense your right leg like you did with your right arm. Include your buttock, hip, thigh, knee, calf, ankle, foot and toes. When you absolutely cannot sense your right leg any longer, bring your attention back to your head again. When your head is full of all that attention, then sense your left leg. Sense your left buttock, hip, thigh, knee, calf, ankle, foot and toes. Sense until failure. Then bring your attention back to the head again. Finally, sense your left arm just like the right arm. Sense your shoulder, upper arm, elbow, forearm, wrist, hand and fingers. Sense the whole of your arm. Hold this sense as long as possible. Then bring the attention back to your head.

When you have finished sensing your right arm, then right leg, then left leg and then left arm in that order only, just be there in that state. Again, you may experience a deeply relaxed state of being with a *sense of wholeness*. Stay in this state as long as possible. Sense the whole of yourself.

When you are ready to end this exercise, slowly take a deep breath. Inhale until you get to point that the lungs are filled, but before you go over into exhalation, hold this breath for a moment and say "I." Notice where the vibration of the word goes inside of you. Then allow your lungs to exhale. Do not be in a hurry. At the end of the exhalation, before your lungs expand and go over into an inhalation, hold this state for a moment and say "am." Repeat the breath control and the "I am" three times. This spreads the energy you have accumulated all over the body. When you are finished, open your eyes and go back into the subjective world.

During the process of this exercise, as in other meditations, you will encounter many obstacles. You may have itches to scratch, the body can be in an uncomfortable posture or you could sneeze or cough. Thoughts may come into your mind, day dreams may take you away and you may even fall asleep or have real dreams. If anything happens to interrupt the sensing, simply come back to the place you lost your attention and continue again.

This is a very important exercise to develop what I call, The Organ of Sense. It is a great help in martial art to develop the sense of the body in postures, stances, beginning position of techniques and the ending position of techniques. It helps in balance. It is especially important in sensing jumping and spinning techniques and the manifestation of force and power.

The depth and breadth of this exercise is the development of your essential essence, your being. The growth of your being will spill over into every aspect of your life and your aim in martial art.

Remember that the Spirit of the Thing is You!

About the Author

James began his martial art journey in 1962, when he and two friends, Jack Hebert and Jimmy Cooksey obtained a book called *This is Karate*, by Masutatsu Oyama. Together they practiced the techniques illustrated in the book in their garages with homemade heavy bags, macawara boards, hanging balls and other unique training aids. Led by Jack, who had some formal training, they sought techniques that had practical fighting application. Like all young, testosterone filled boys they often got in to fights and even gang fights in their rough city of Port Arthur, Texas. Their heroes back then were Bruce Lee, Chuck Norris, Bill Wallace, Mike Stone and Ed Parker. In addition they practiced Ninja skills like climbing buildings, fence walking, stealth hiding and all sorts of unusual and sometime dangerous endeavors at night while avoiding the police cruisers.

When James got older his martial art experience was put on hold. He went to college and obtained three degrees – chemistry, biology and pharmacy. He also was a flight instructor, appliance repairman, a plumber and was skilled in all the building trades. When he got married, he and his wife Sherry felt something was missing from their lives and attended The Institute for Religious Development in Warwick, New York. Here, they spent many years absorbing and practicing an ancient teaching that had been lost to mankind. Part of this teaching was the practice of sacred dances that were found in remote monasteries. These dances, which they simply called "movements," were handed down from generation to generation, unchanged for thousands of years.

When James and Sherry decided to start a family, they moved back to Texas and settled in the city of Bryan. Here, they were disappointed by the absence of spiritual practice they had known in New York. They realized that some aspects of martial art, especially forms, were "three centered activities" similar to the sacred movements they had practiced at the Institute. They wanted their children to experience the benefits of this type of activity. When their daughter Laura was twelve and their son Joey was nine, they enrolled them in a taekwondo school in Bryan. The school was affiliated with the American Taekwondo Association (ATA).

After several months, their children were having so much fun, James and Sherry decided to join taekwondo also. James was forty-four and Sherry was forty. Because their children were two belts ahead of them, they helped their parents learn martial art. The Killingworth's became the first Black Belt family in their local association. When Laura and Joey went into high school they left their practice of martial art behind. Laura went into gymnastics and Joey went into baseball and football.

James and Sherry continued their journey in taekwondo. They built their own dojang (place of formal exercise) in their back yard and practiced together on a regular basis. After a period of hesitation, they both decided to enter into competition. As they continued to ascend through Black Belt ranks, they both earned the title of World Champions. Sherry won eight Top Ten Medals and two World Titles. James won thirty-one Top Ten Medals and fifteen World Titles. Sherry obtained the rank of Fourth Degree Black Belt and James was a Fifth Degree Black Belt.

In James' final year of competition (2015), he swept his entire division (60-99 year olds). He won first place in all four events – forms, sparring, weapons and combat weapons. This earned him four World Titles (Gold Medals) and the coveted Quadruple Crown. He was sixty-eight years old. Since they achieved all of their aims in martial art competition, they decided to retire. He and his wife still train together in their own dojang and are now training their grandson.

Black Belt Family
1994

Dual World Champions
2012

Attitude

"No, no, no, not hot enough!" Master M. K. Lee smiled and handed the choko (cup) of Sake back to Mrs. Rogers. The process was repeated twice again before he smiled, nodded and said "good." A small man by American standard, he was of medium stature. Yet his carriage was erect, his movements sure and cat-like. His attentive countenance examined every face, every voice, every posture and gesture. His courtesy was in each answer to all questions, no matter how superficial. He continued every conversation in its indicated direction, fluidly moving in and out of awkward situations. At first mundane, the jokes started to flow freely like the Sake. Then they became raucous and were punctured by roars of laughter until Sherry jabbed her elbow into my ribs and reminded me to behave myself. The conversation rambled through many subjects - parrots, food, tournaments, guns and then to taekwondo. This dinner party at Mr. and Mrs. Rogers' house, our taekwondo instructors, was the culmination of the Rogers first local tournament (Brazos Blow Out II in 1993) at College Station, Texas. Master M. K., as we called him, had come to support them and meet their students. The Rogers had a huge Macaw named Hondo, whose cage was in the living room. He squawked loudly when we laughed and he always kept his eye on us.

Partially paralyzed by the fajitas and Mexican cuisine, the Sake lowered our inhibitions and the conversation begin to take on more meaning. I was starting to forget the aches and pains in my ball and socket joints after fighting Bill in the tournament just a few hours earlier. Bill and Ruth Watson were with us at the party. The Watsons were our friends and students in our school.

We began to realize that this man in front of us had knowledge and understanding that dreams are made of. Yet we would have to come to him before he would share it. My voice changed, my mind cleared and I vowed that I would not let this moment pass in silence.

"Master Lee, I am having a problem with a certain segment in Red Belt form. I can never get it right. Whenever I do it I lose my balance." As he listened to me his demeanor changed, almost as if he was relieved that someone had asked him a question from the heart.

"Let me see," he said.

There in the Rogers' living room, between the Macaw and the coffee table I performed. Double knife-hand low block, extended upset ridge-hand strike, reverse hook kick, stumble, adjustment, reverse punch and ridge-hand strike. Sheepishly, I returned to my seat. Even as a Black Belt Recommended, I could not get through that segment without screwing it up. No wonder I did not place in forms competition at the tournament.

His eyes pierced deeply into mine to see if he had my attention and then simply said, "You have wrong attitude." The shock of his words struck my feelings a heavy blow, yet my mind was puzzled. Wrong attitude? I thought to myself, in my gross way, that a person either had a good or bad attitude. What was a wrong attitude?

"You have already accepted that you are going to do this segment wrong, and each time you do it you just try to get through it and go on to the rest of the form. This is wrong attitude toward learning form."

Suddenly Master Lee was in the middle of the living room. Hondo watched warily as the Sixth Degree Black Belt performed this Red Belt segment between his perch and the couch. Rear stance, chamber high, double knife-hand low block, middle stance, inverted ridge-hand strike, guard position, head and hips turn, legs cross, chamber, hook kick, rechamber, back stance, reverse punch and ridge-hand strike. I turned to catch Ruth and Sherry's eyes as their astonishment verified that we had witnessed this segment to perfection. Each move was crisp and precise, yet flowing effortlessly and ending with a powerful snap amid total balance.

Master Lee sat back down and peered at me again.

"You must break down each move into its component parts and visualize them in perfection. Then practice until it becomes how you have visualized it. Do not accept less. Get Mr. or Mrs. Rogers to perform this form for you, so you can see it in perfection and have that image to practice toward. Always strive for perfection." He paused for a moment to allow his words to find their proper place inside of me and then added. "This is right attitude," he assured me.

It was as if an explosion of silence cleaned away all of the delusions inside of me. He had struck deep. In an instant, he not only showed me the error of my way, but that it spilled over into the very way I had approached my life, my work, my play and the way I pursued my goals.

I felt a deep sense about what taekwondo and the association with such a man could mean for me in the course of my life. If taekwondo could produce a man like this, then I was ready to take that path.

"There is more, you must focus. Look before you strike, especially when you turn. You must see where you are moving to or you will be out of control. Focus is an important quality of technique and balance. It delivers your power to a precise point. This is all written down. I will send you a copy if you wish."

As the evening wore on we all opened up to this marvelous man with our questions and problems in taekwondo. Many answers were given and we all benefited from his presence. Like a great meal, it would take some time for us to digest and assimilate all of that evening's value.

He arose, stretched and disappeared into the kitchen, returning with the last choko of Sake. He deftly placed it before me and slowly turned it in a ritualistic way. Our eyes met and he bowed to me.

Attitude

Appendix/Bibliography

1. Chapter 1

   The Eye of Revelation: The Ancient Tibetan Rites of Rejuvenation by Peter Kelder.

2. Chapter 2

   Life Extension: A Practical Scientific Approach by Durk Pearson and Sandy Shaw.

   Life Extension Foundation-lef.org

   10-Day Detox Diet by Mark Hyman, M.D.

   Reverse Heart Disease Now by Stephen T. Sinatra, M.D. and James C. Roberts, M.D.

   The Arthritis Cure by Jason Theodosakis, M.D. and Sheila Buff.

   Eat To Live by Joel Fuhrman, M.D.

3. Chapter 3

   Dynamic Stretching and Kicking by Bill Wallace.

   Stretching Scientifically by Thomas Kurz.

4. Chapter 4

   Dr. Scholl's Mole Foam Pads (UPC 14900).

5. Chapter 5

   In Search of the Miraculous by P. D. Ouspensky.

   Meetings with Remarkable Men by G. I. Gurdjieff.

6. Chapter 8

   Outside Magazine: January 1999, Bodywork.

   Jumping Into Plyometrics by Donald A. Chu.

7. Chapter 9

    Taekwondo Drills for Modern Competition Sparring, a video by Dana Hee.

8. Chapter 10

    This is Karate by Masutatsu Oyama.

9. Chapter 11

    Tao of Jeet Kune Do - The Way of the Intercepting Fist by Bruce Lee.

10. Chapter 12

    The Book of Five Rings by Miyamoto Musashi, translated by William Scott Wilson.

    The Ten Attributes, taught by the American Taekwondo Association.

    The Ole Man: Episodes of the Heart by James Killingsworth.